Jazz Guitar Workshop Book I

Daily Warm Up Exercises
for
Guitar

Methods
for
developing a daily practice routine
with
scales, modes & arpeggios.

Guitar Tab Edition

by Robert Green

1st Edition October 2013

Print Edition   ISBN 978-1-937187-01-9
eBook Edition ISBN 978-1-937187-04-0

Library of Congress Control Number:

Musical Score : Fretted instruments & guitar
Musical Score : Studies & exercises, etudes

Layout and music engraving by Robert Green
Cover Design by Robert Green

Table of Contents.

Table of Contents.

Foreward

Jazz Guitar Workshop Book I - Daily Warm Up Exercieses for Guitar.

Guitar Method for developing a dedicated daily practice routine utilising scales, modes & arpeggios.

One of the most important aspects of learning any instrument is being able to set aside time to practice.
Even if you have only 30 min per day, by organising your time and having the dedication to follow through
with your plan, progress is yours to be had.
All exercises in this book are given in guitar tab and treble clef enabling guitarists of all levels and musical
backgrounds to have access to musical exercises that help to build instrumental facility and musicianship.
Have the dedication to practice the exercises slowly, working on good time, tone and intonation.
As a wise instructor once said, " there's no magic powder ".
Great players worked hard to get there, if it is your wish and your intention, you can get there too.

All exercises are provided in 12 keys. For the advanced student, practice the book in 12 keys, for the
beginning to intermediate student practice the exercises in one key to gain familiarity with the instrument.
When the exercises become comfortable move to another key until all keys are comfortable.

Scale studies are designed to help the guitarist to learn the fingerboard while building dexterity, flexibilty,
stamina as well as building muscle memory and training the ear.

The exercises in this book are practiced by professional musicians of all backgrounds, from rock to jazz to
classiscal musicians.

This book is designed for the beginning to intermediate guitarist.
It is advised that the beginning guitarist use the book under the guidance of an experienced guitar teacher
to accelerate the learning process.

SCALE STUDIES IN THE KEY OF C MAJOR

C major scale 2 octaves

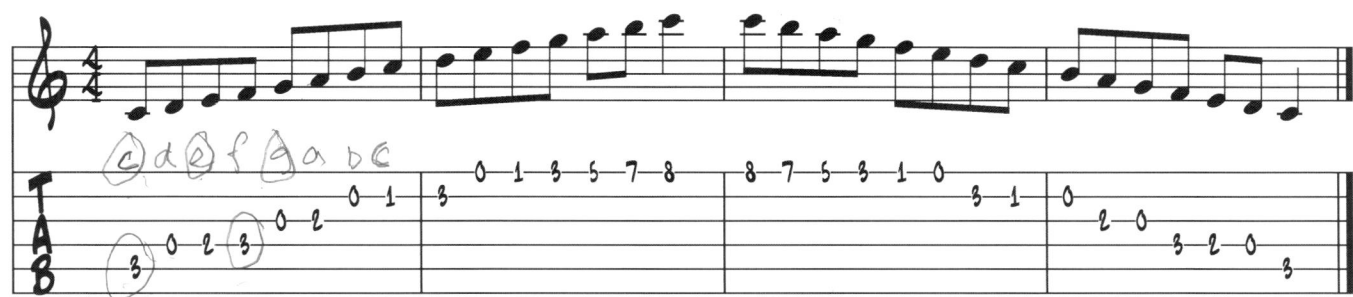

C major 7 arpeggio 2 octaves

D Dorian scale 2 octaves

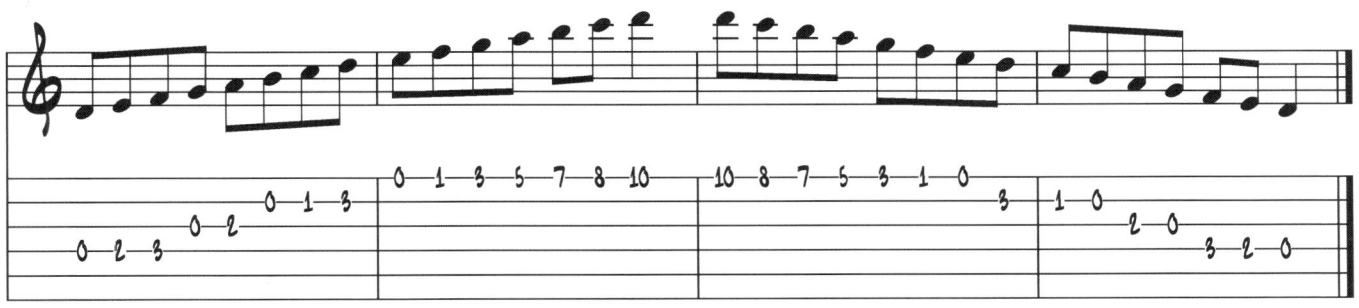

D min 7 arpeggio 2 octaves

E Phrygian scale

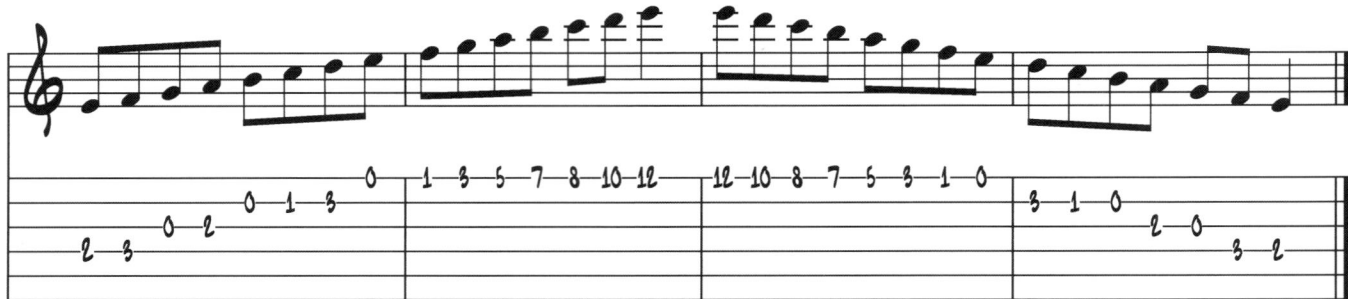

E min 7 arpeggio

F Lydian scale

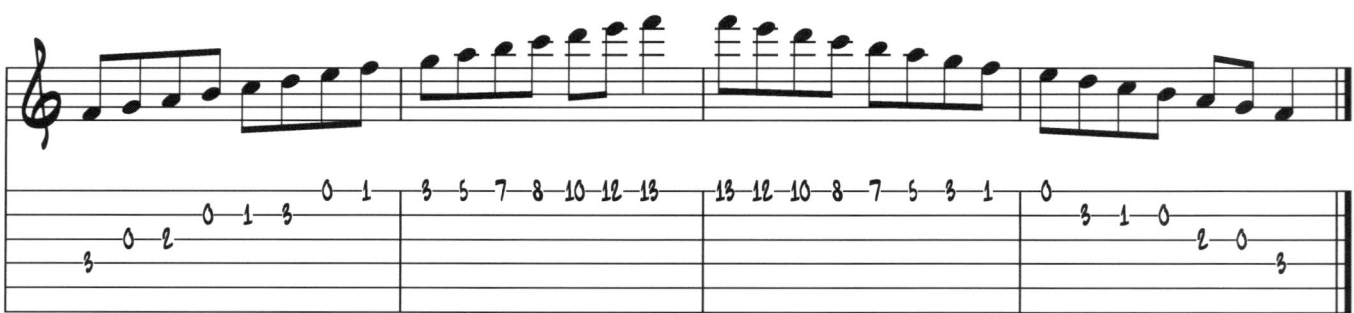

F maj 7 arpeggio

G Mixolydian scale

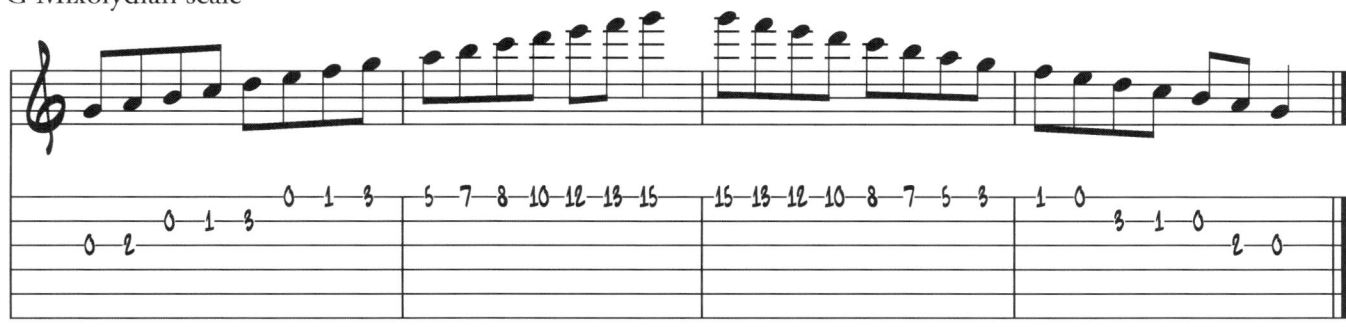

G 7 arpeggio

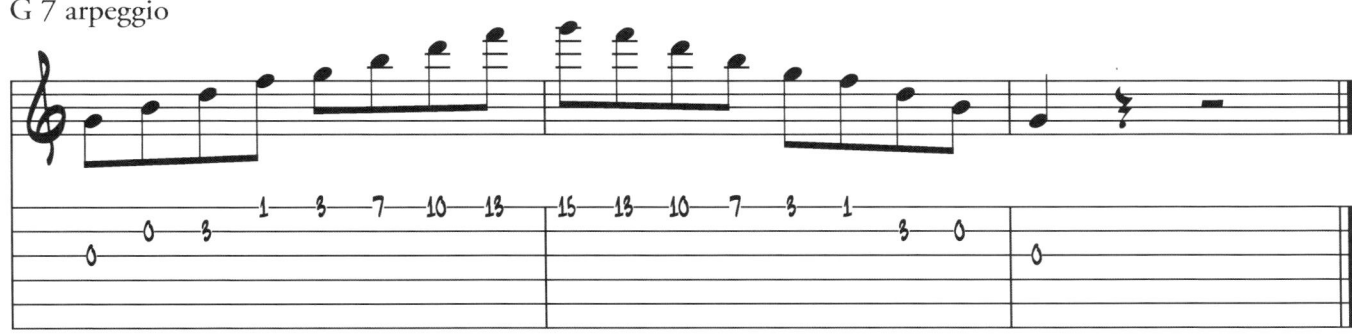

A Aeolian scale

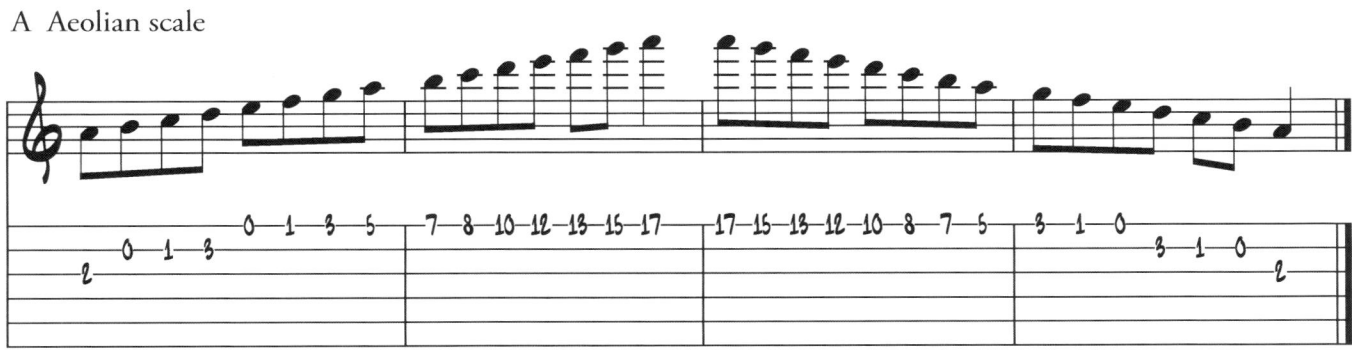

A min7 arpeggio

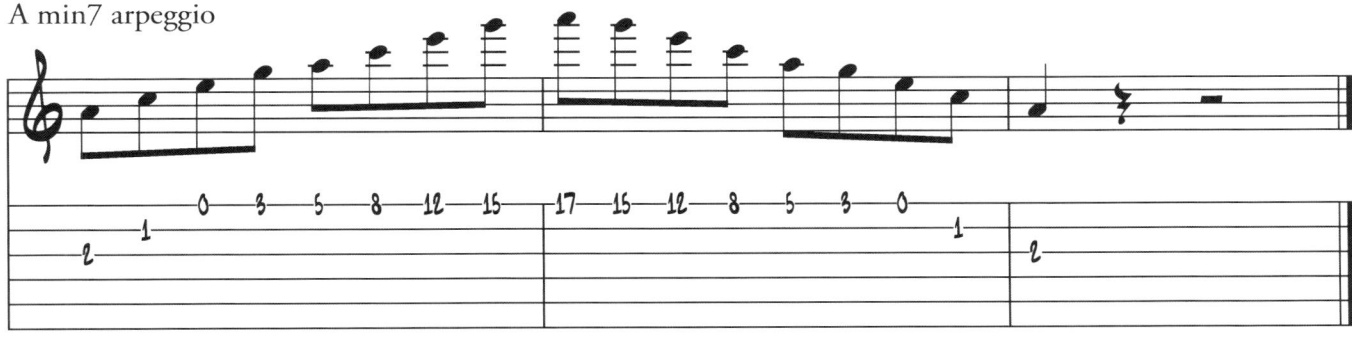

B Locrian scale

B min7 b5 arpeggio

4 Note Scale Groupings

The following exercise outlines the use of 4 note groupings moving stepwise diatonically through the scale of C major.

For example, the 4 note grouping starts on the root note or 1st degree of the scale and progresses stepwise. The exercise then descends from the 2nd octave C back to the root.

Ascending

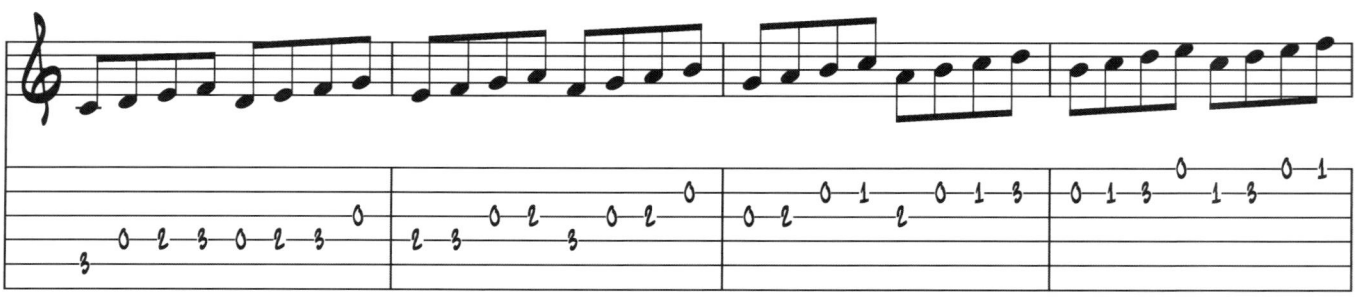

Descending

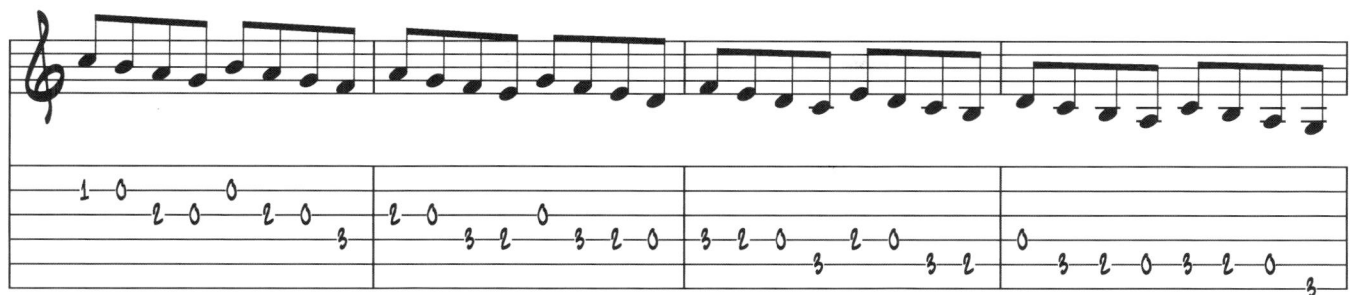

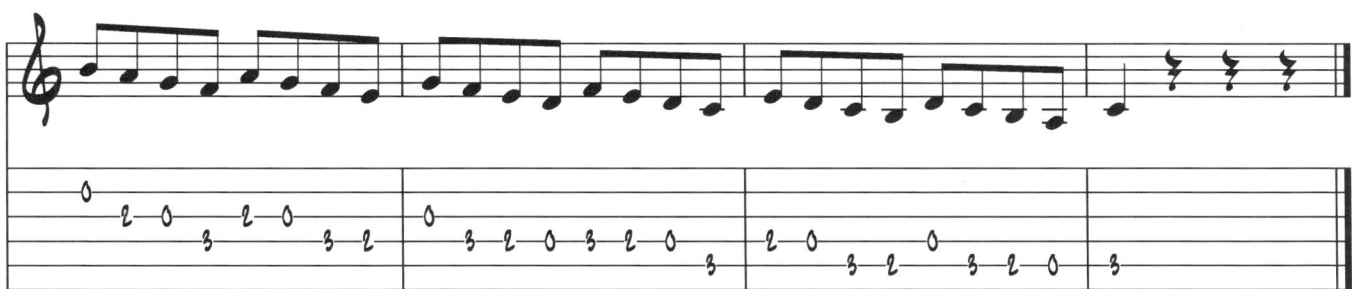

Permutation 2   Up & Down

As in the previous exercise the following exercise outlines the use of 4 note groupings moving stepwise diatonically through the scale of C major.

Notice in exercise #2 the 4 note grouping starts on the root note or 1st degree of the scale and progresses stepwise. In this example we descend when we hit the 5th note in the sequence eg. descending from the 2nd 4 note grouping.

Ascending

Descending

BROKEN THIRDS

Ascending

Descending

4 Note Groupings Diatonic Triads

Ascending 1351

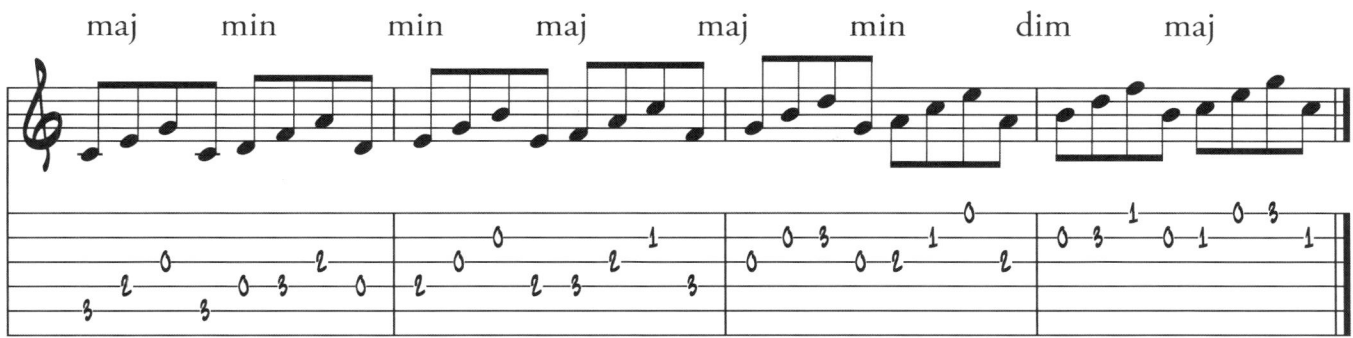

Descending 1351

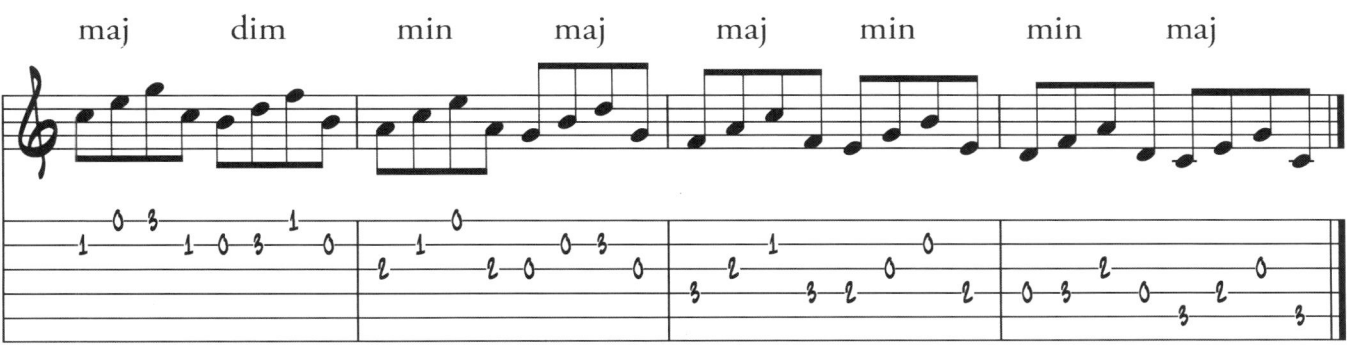

Ascending 1531

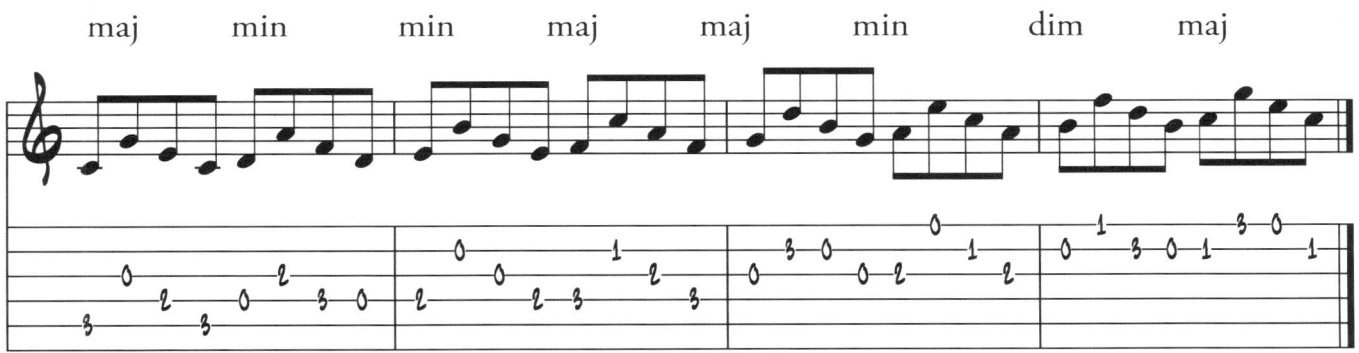

Descending 1531

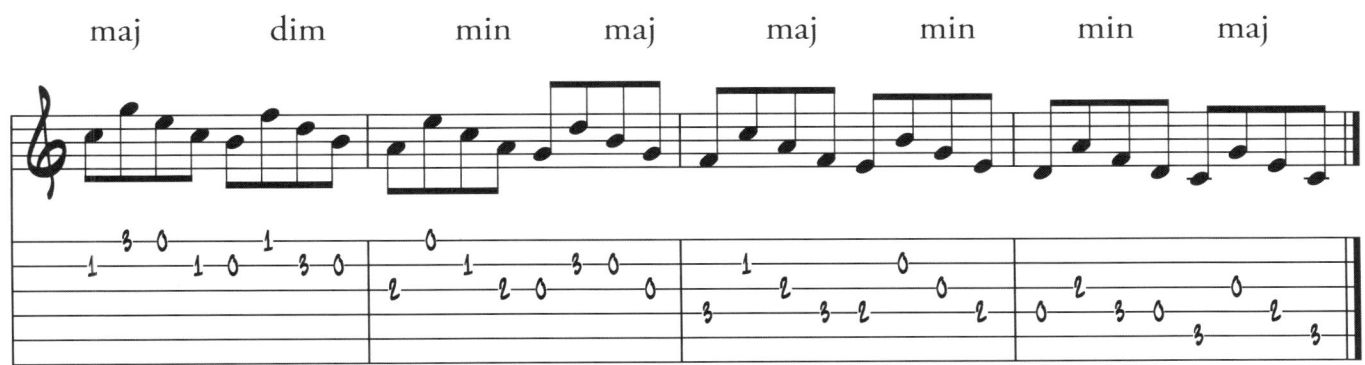

4 Note Groupings Diatonic 7th Chords

Ascending

Descending

4 Note Groupings Diatonic 7th Chords

Permutation 2
Ascending & descending

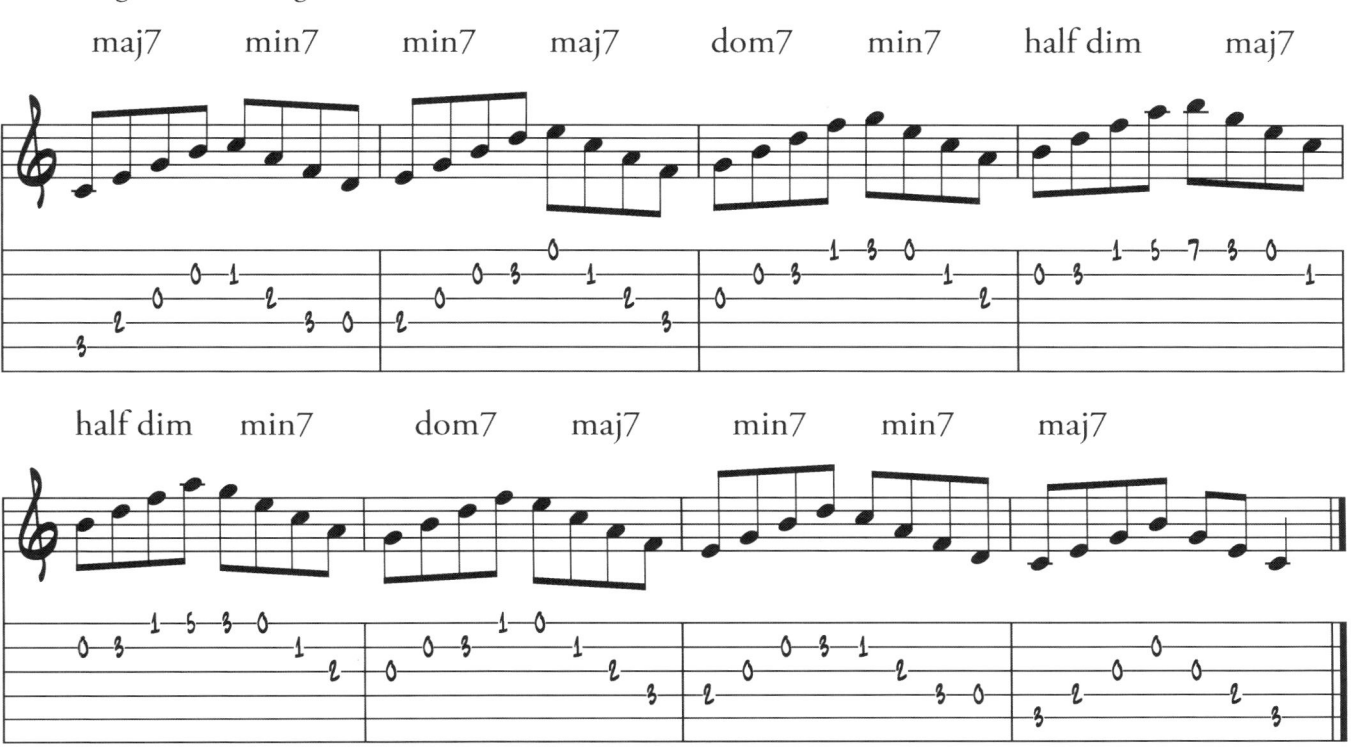

Permutation 3
Down the chord stepwise up the scale

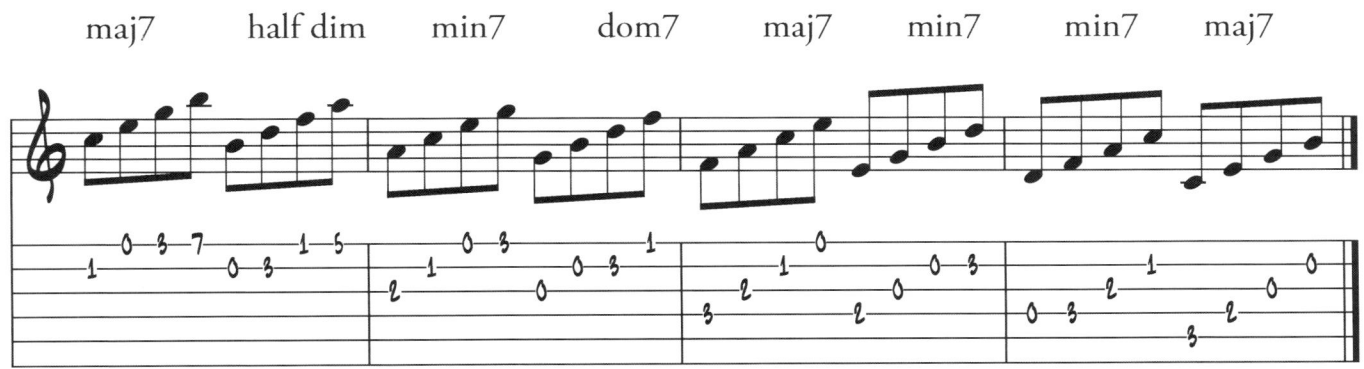

3 Note Groupings

C major scale in triplet groupings
Ascending

Descending

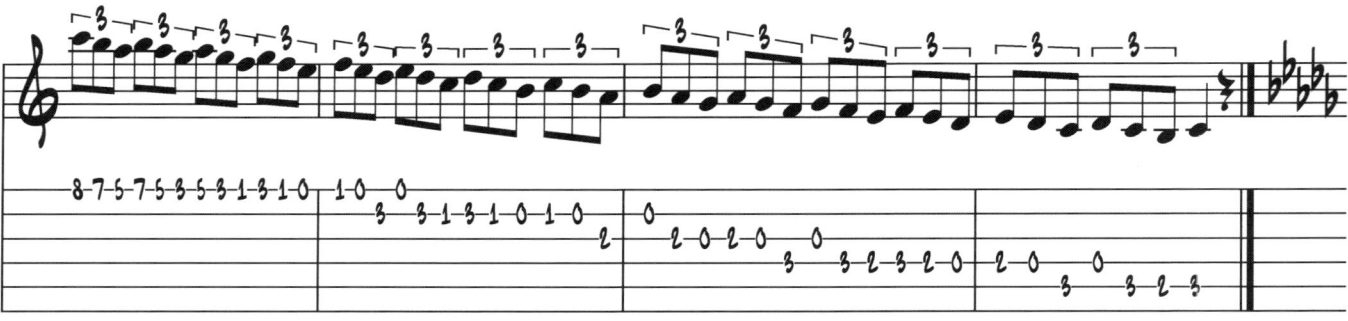

Scale studies in the key of Db Major

Db Major scale

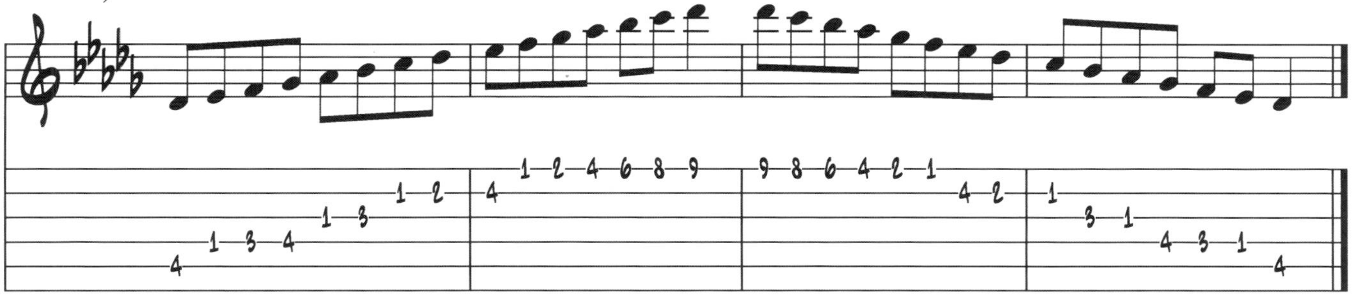

Db maj7 arpeggio

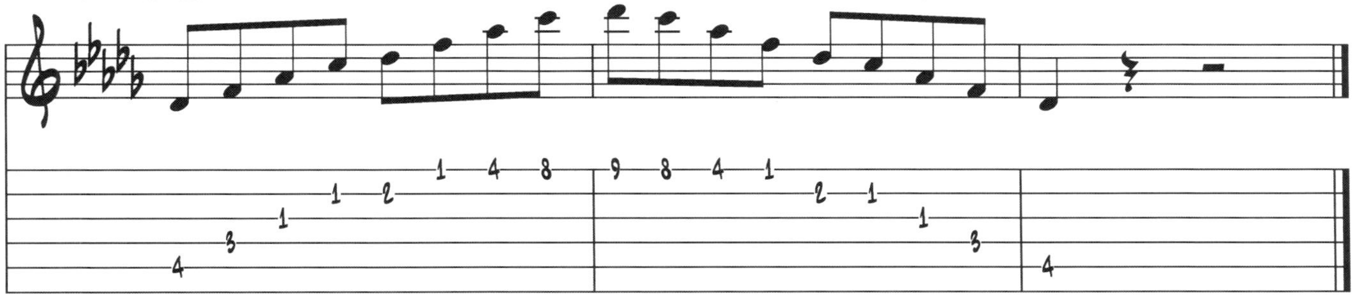

Eb Dorian scale

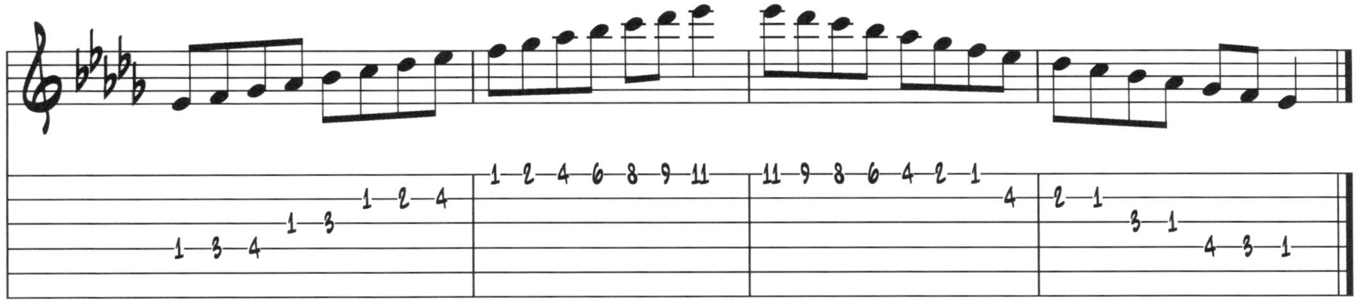

Eb min7 arpeggio

F Phrygian scale

F min7 arpeggio

Gb Lydian scale

Gb maj7 arpeggio

Ab Mixolydian scale

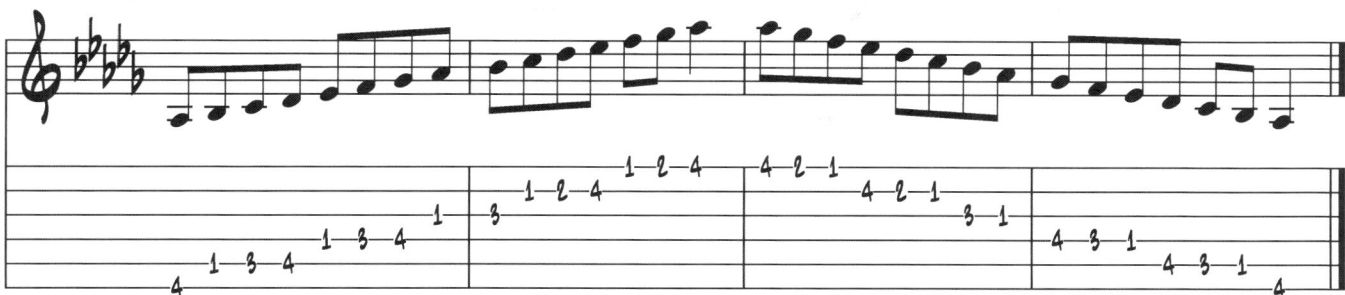

Ab7 arpeggio

Bb Aeolian scale

Bb min7 arpeggio

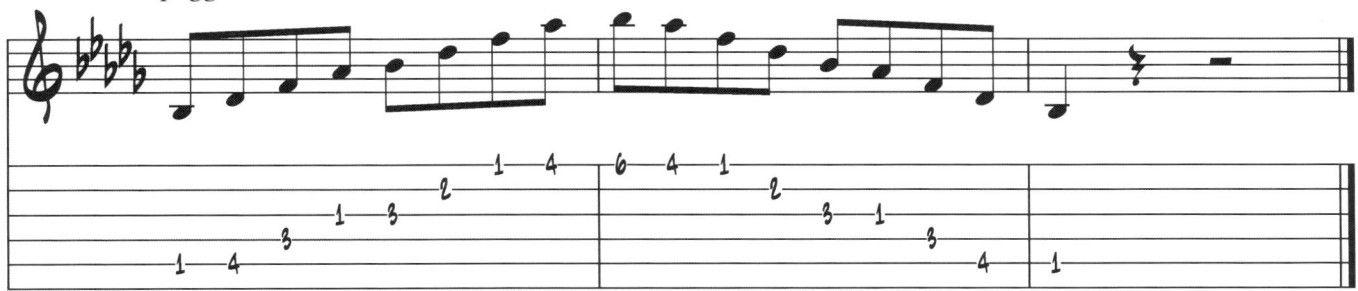

C Locrian scale

C min7 b5 arpeggio

4 Note Scale Groupings

The following exercise outlines the use of 4 note groupings moving stepwise diatonically through the scale of Db major.

For example, the 4 note grouping starts on the root note or 1st degree of the scale and progresses stepwise. The exercise then descends from the 2nd octave Db back to the root.

Ascending

Descending

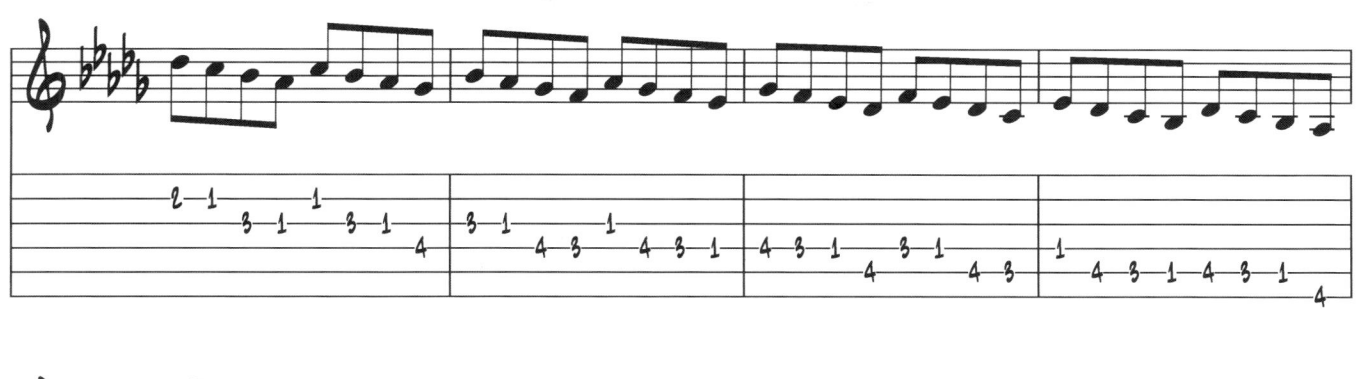

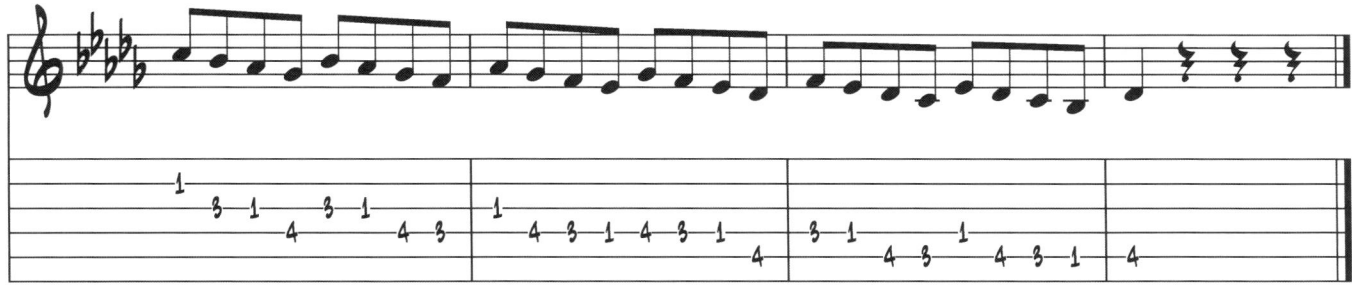

Permutation 2   Up & Down

As in the previous exercise the following exercise outlines the use of 4 note groupings moving stepwise diatonically through the scale of Db major.

Notice in exercise #2 the 4 note grouping starts on the root note or 1st degree of the scale and progresses stepwise. In this example we descend when we hit the 5th note in the sequence eg. descending from the 2nd 4 note grouping.

Ascending

Descending

Broken Thirds

Ascending

Descending

4 Note Groupings Diatonic Triads

4 Note Groupings Diatonic 7th Chords

Permutation 2
Ascending & descending

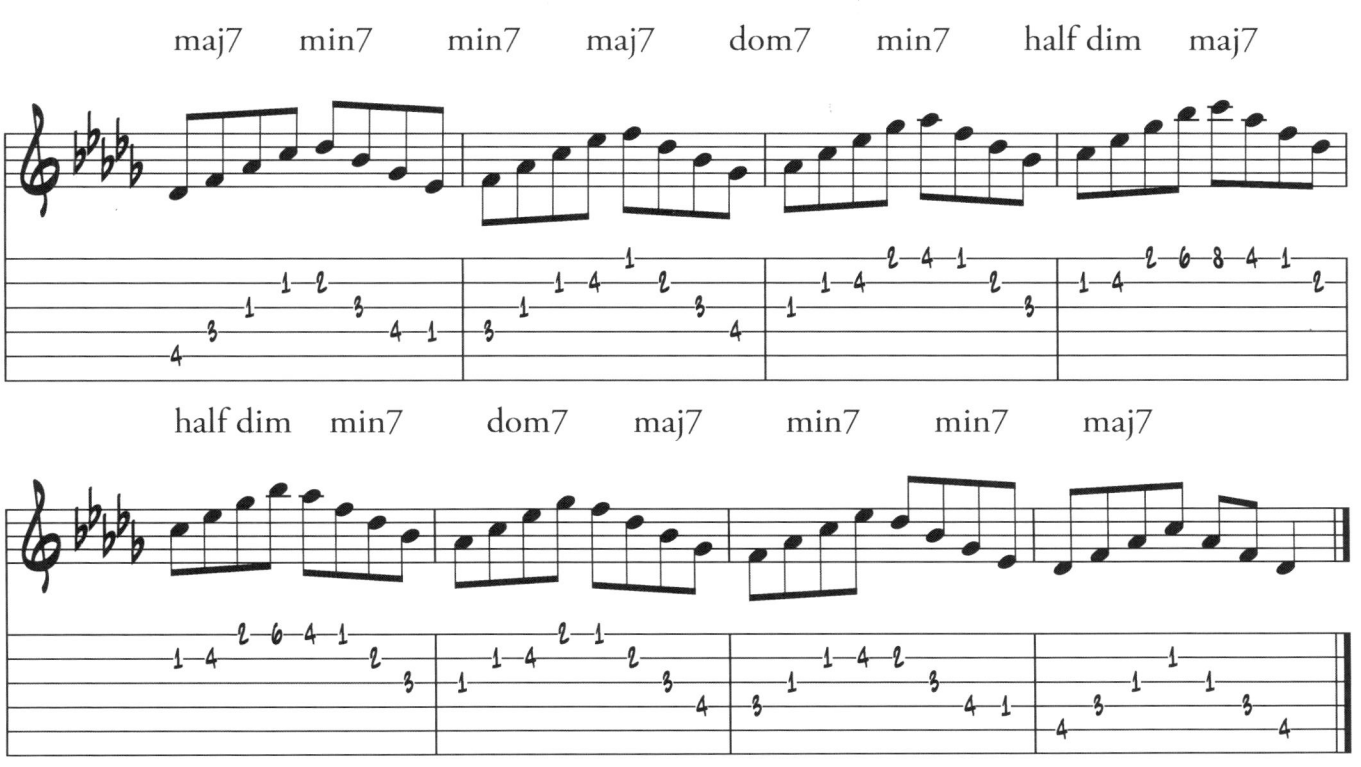

Permutation 3
Down the chord stepwise up the scale

3 Note Groupings

Db major scale in triplet groupings
Ascending

Descending

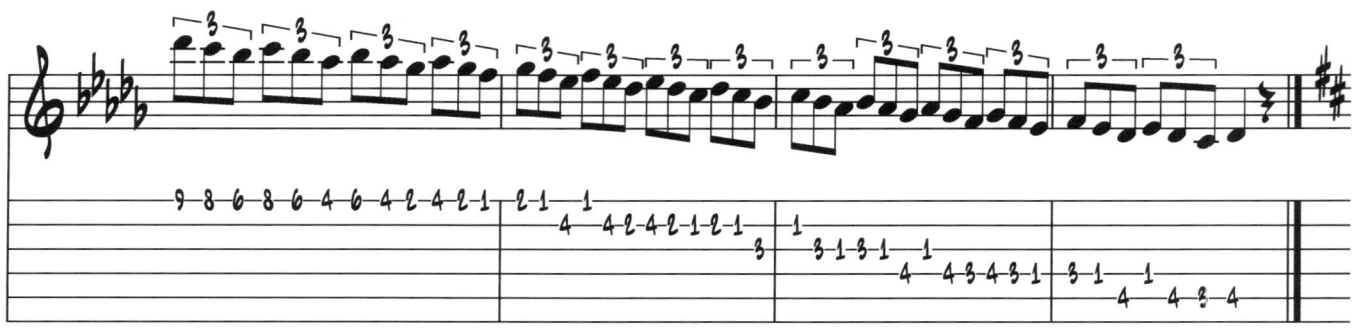

Scale studies in the key of D Major

Scales, Modes and Arpeggios over 2 octaves

D Major 7 scale

D maj 7 arpeggio

E Dorian scale

E min7 arpeggio

F# Phrygian scale

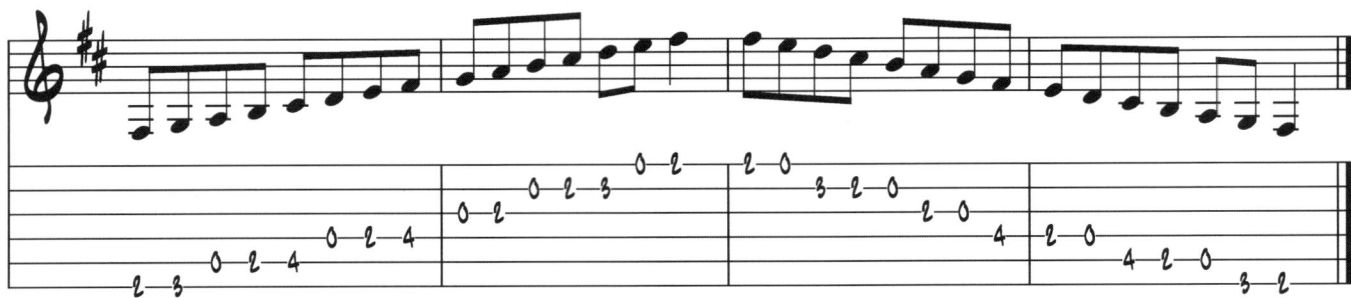

F# min7 arpeggio

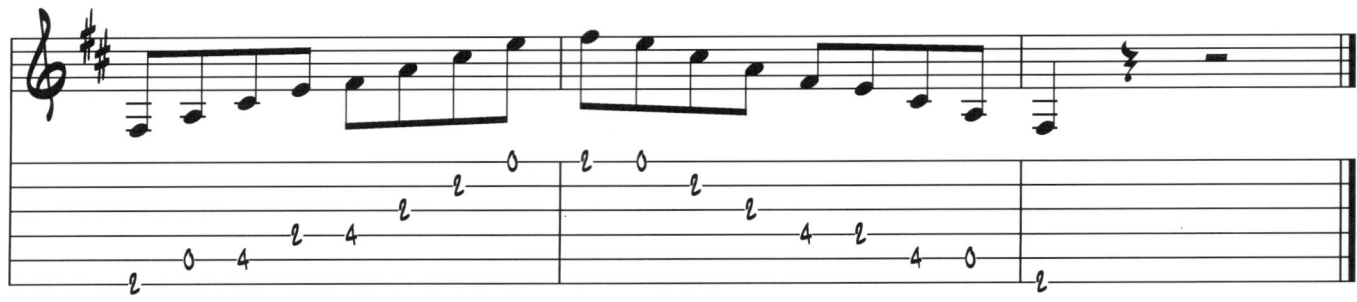

G Lydian scale

G maj 7 arpeggio

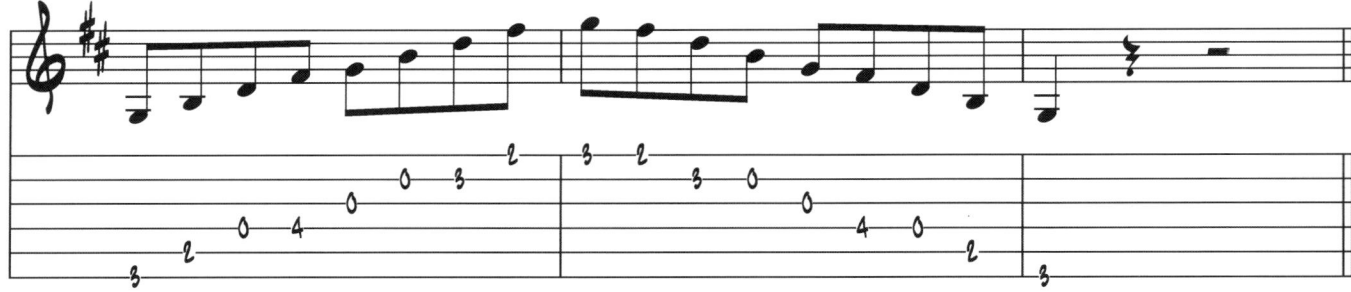

A Mixolydian scale

A dom7 arpeggio

B Aeolian scale

B min7 arpeggio

C# Locrian scale

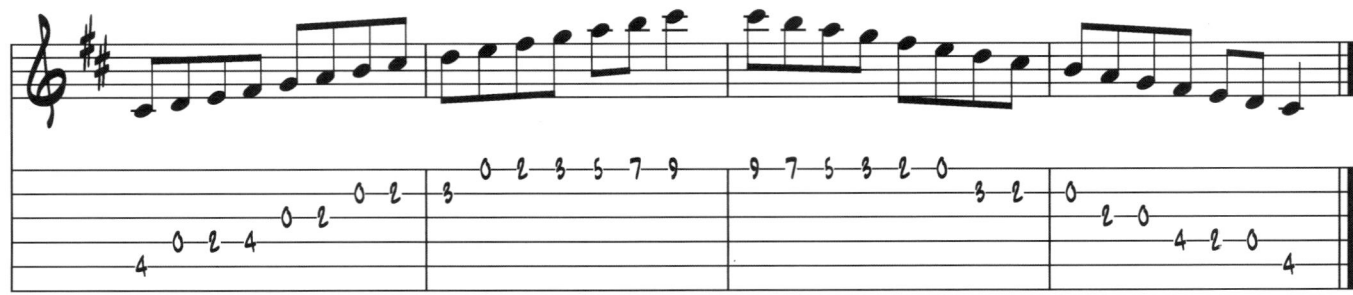

C# min7 b5 arpeggio

4 Note Scale Groupings

The following exercise outlines the use of 4 note groupings moving stepwise diatonically through the scale of D major.

For example, the 4 note grouping starts on the root note or 1st degree of the scale and progresses stepwise. The exercise then descends from the 2nd octave D back to the root.

Ascending

Descending

Permutation 2   Up & Down

As in the previous exercise the following exercise outlines the use of 4 note groupings moving stepwise diatonically through the scale of D major.

Notice in exercise #2 the 4 note grouping starts on the root note or 1st degree of the scale and progresses stepwise. In this example we descend when we hit the 5th note in the sequence eg. descending from the 2nd 4 note grouping.

Ascending

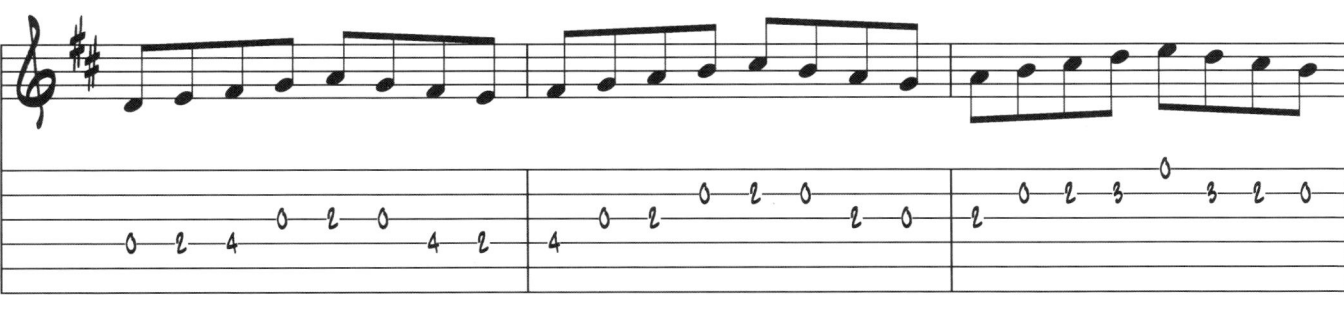

Descending

Broken Thirds

Ascending

Descending

4 Note Groupings Diatonic Triads

Ascending 1351

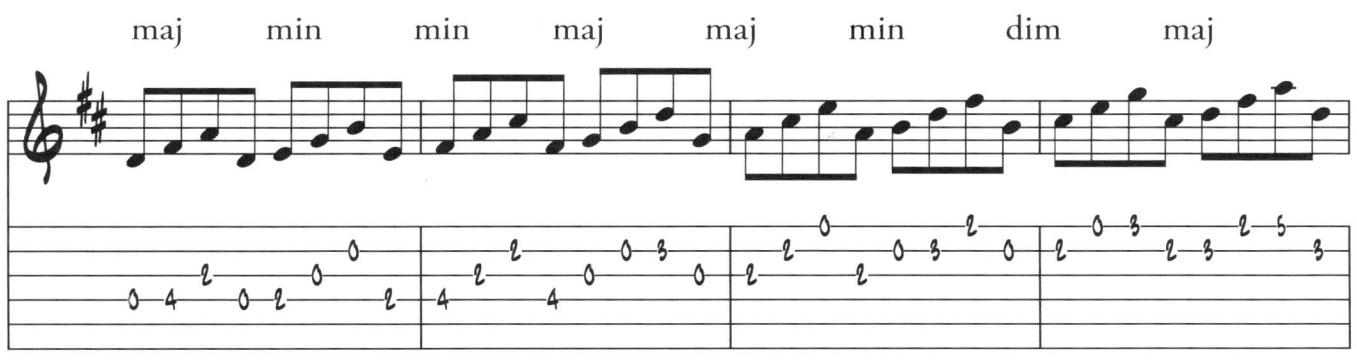

Descending 1351

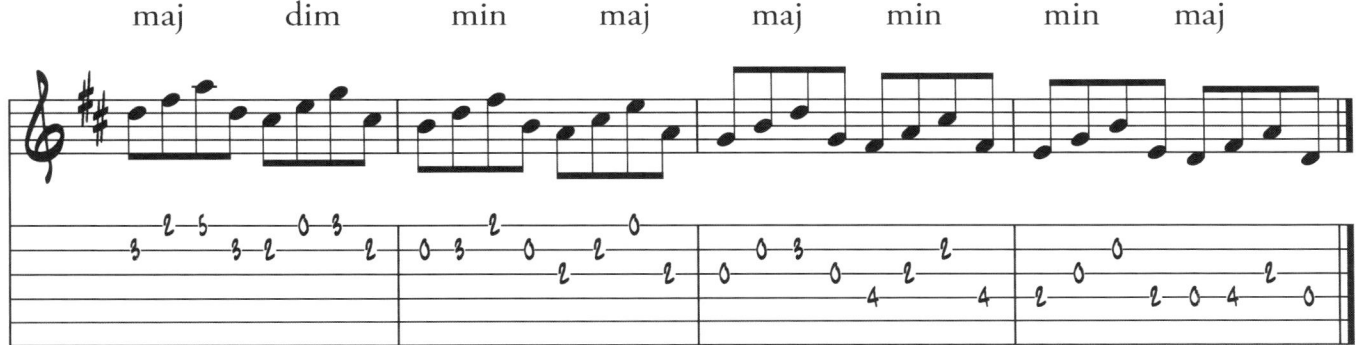

Ascending 1531

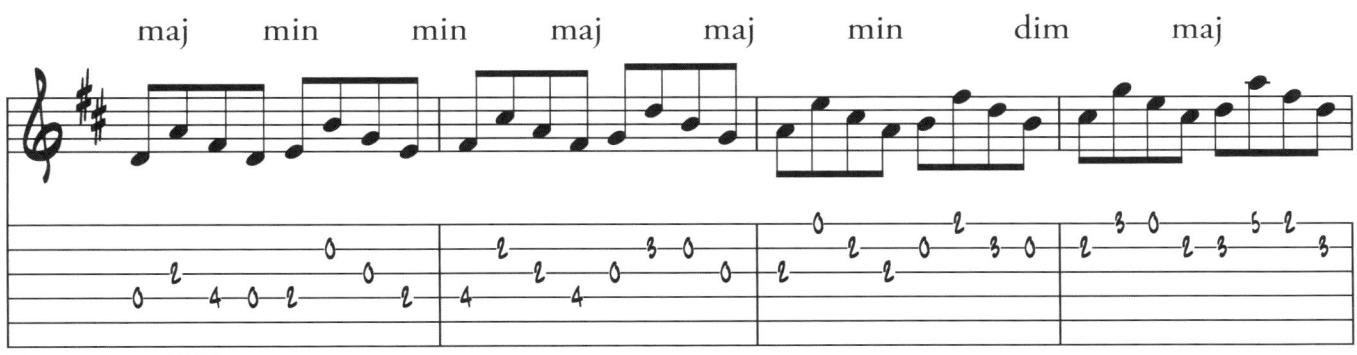

Descending 1531

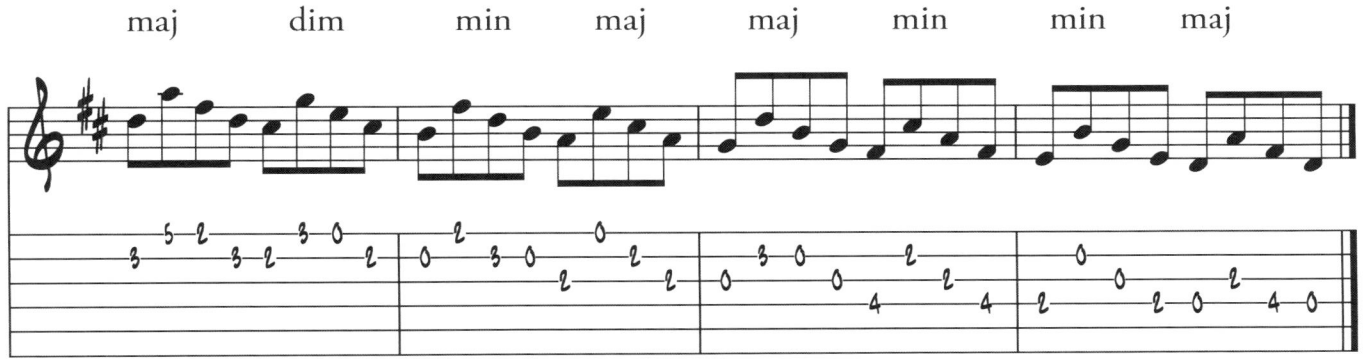

4 Note Groupings Diatonic 7th chords

Ascending

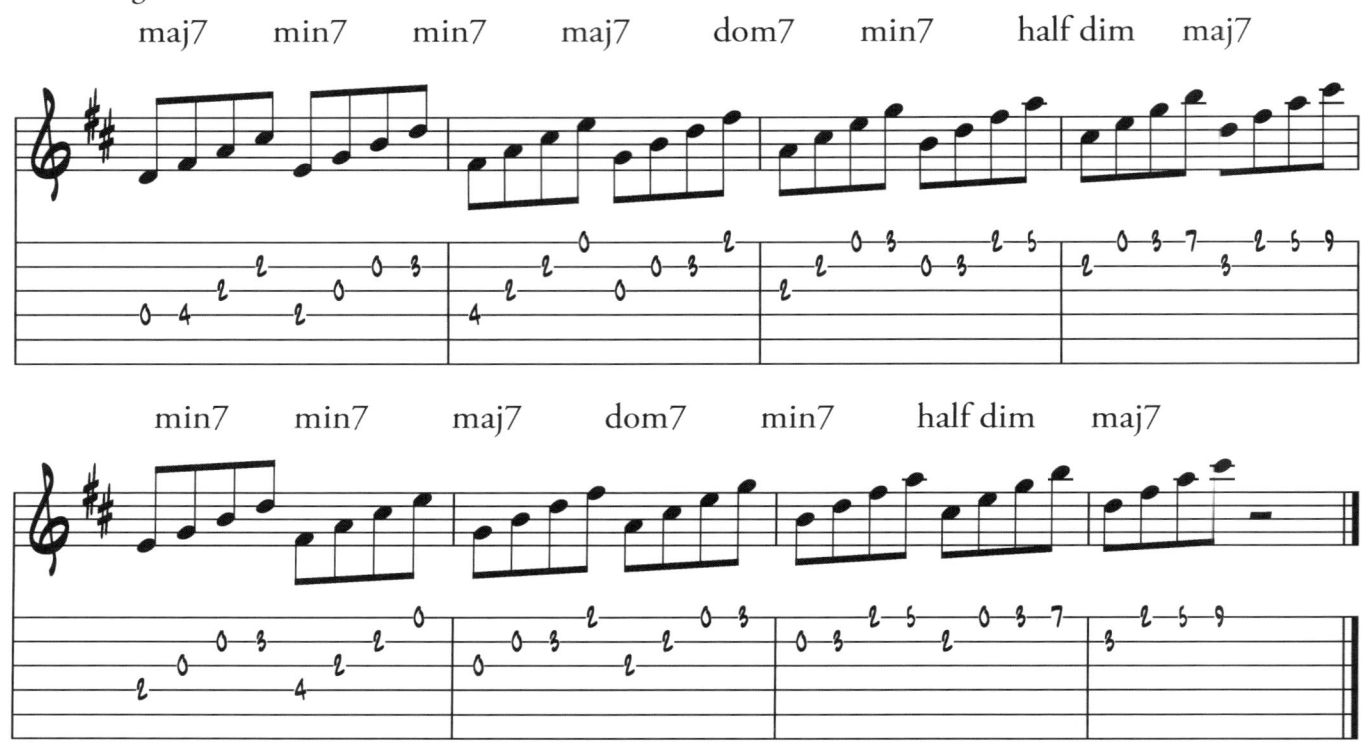

Descending

Permutation 2
Ascending & descending

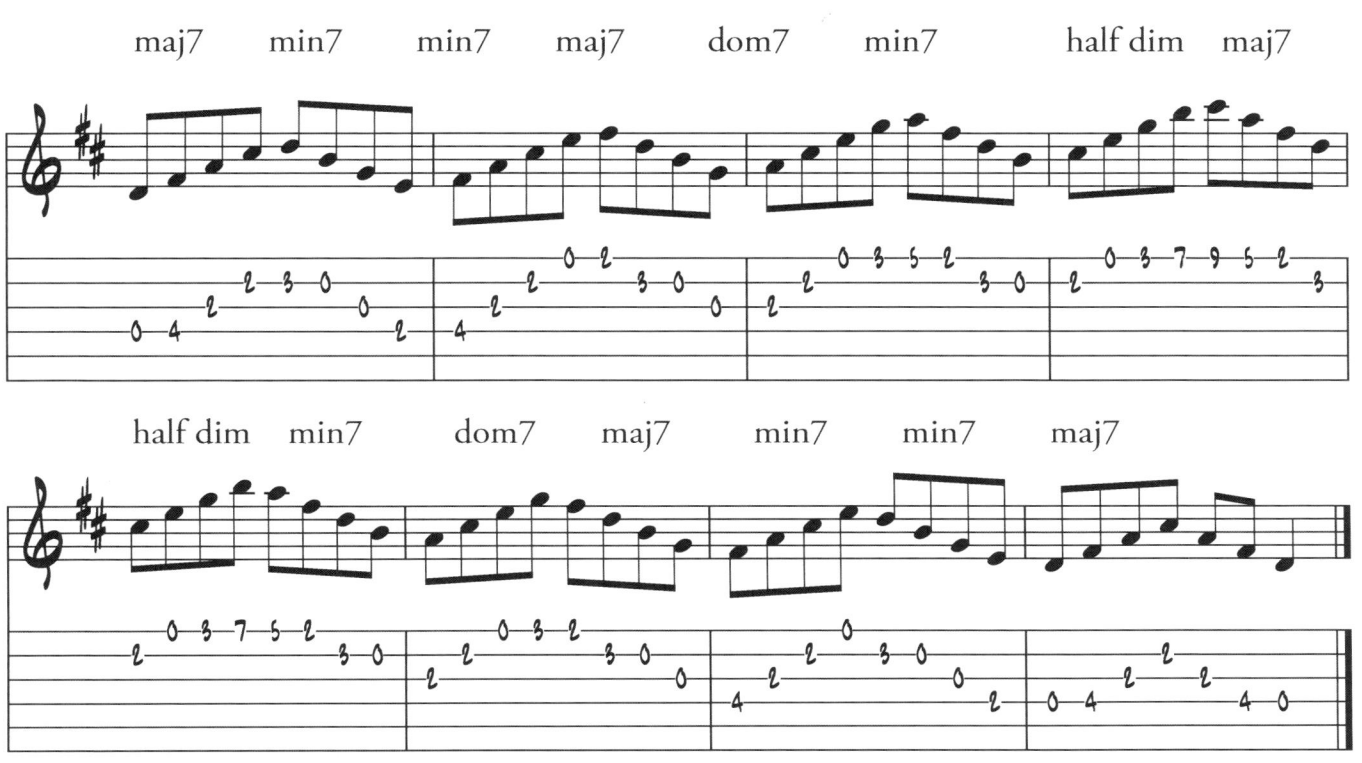

Permutation 3
Down the chord stepwise up the scale

3 Note Groupings

D major scale in triplet groupings
Ascending

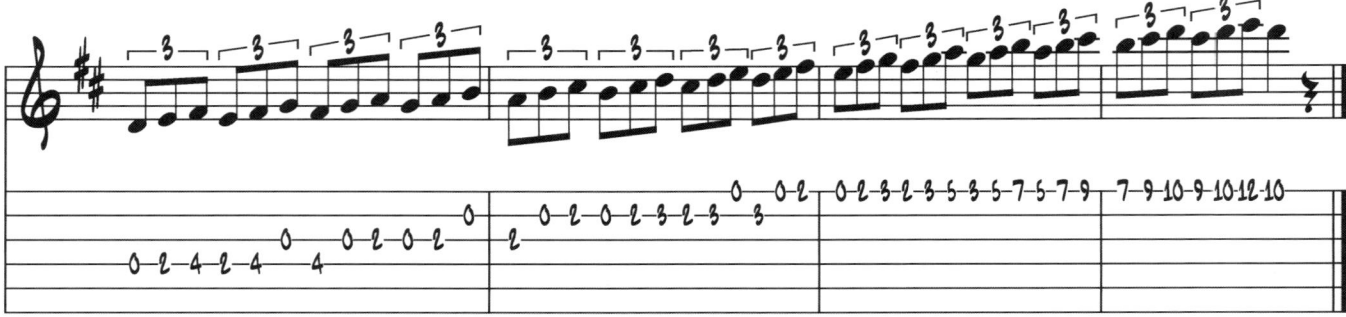

Descending

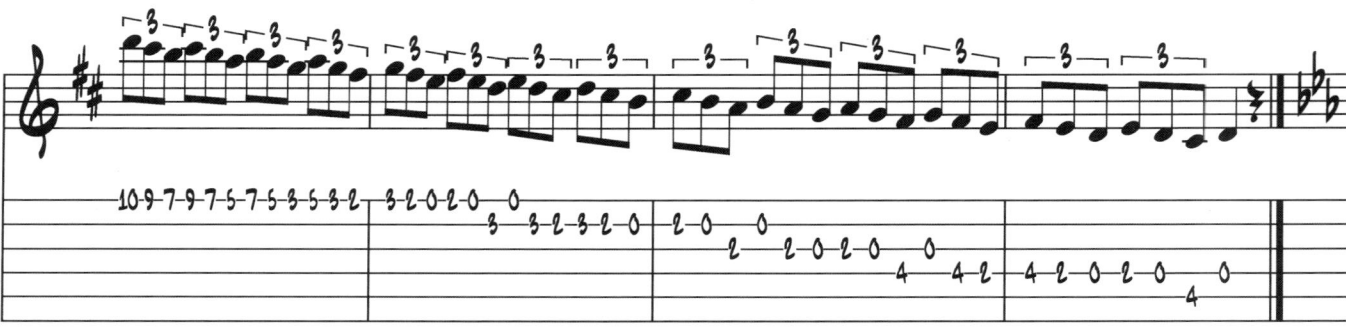

Scale studies in the key of Eb Major

Scales, Modes and Arpeggios over 2 octaves

Eb Major scale

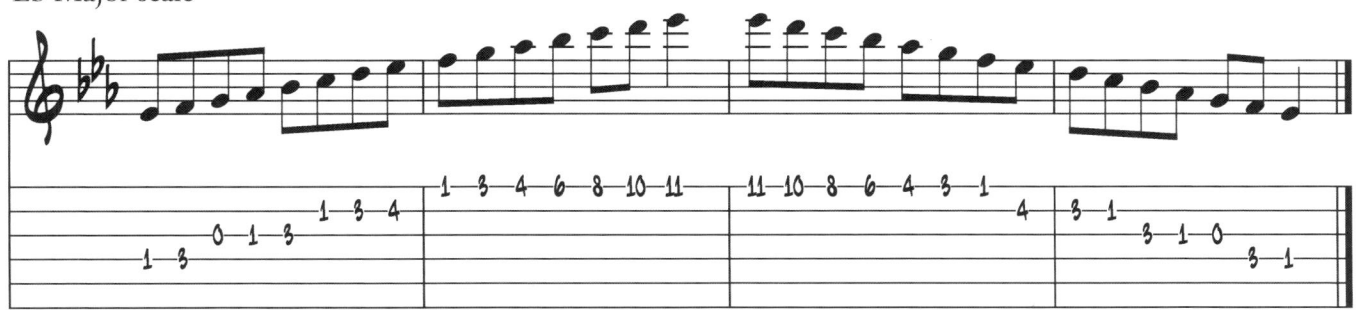

Eb maj 7 arpeggio

F Dorian scale

F min 7 arpeggio

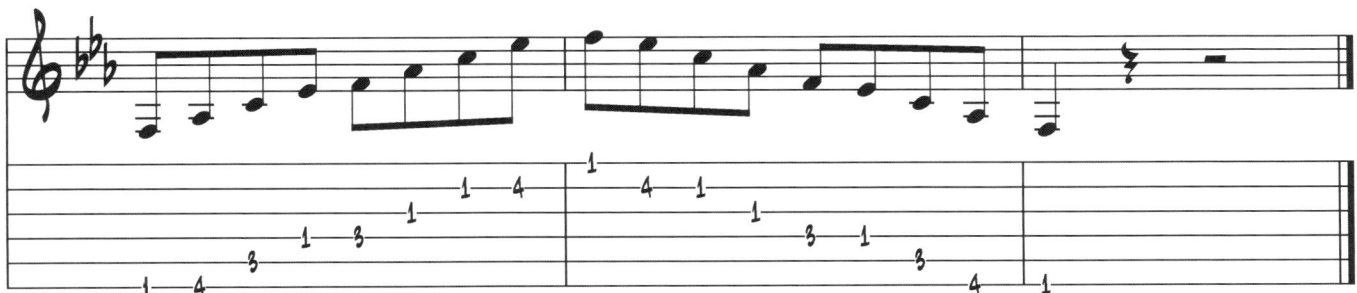

G Phrygian scale

G min 7 arpeggio

Ab Lydian scale

Ab maj 7 arpeggio

Bb Mixolydian scale

Bb7 arpeggio

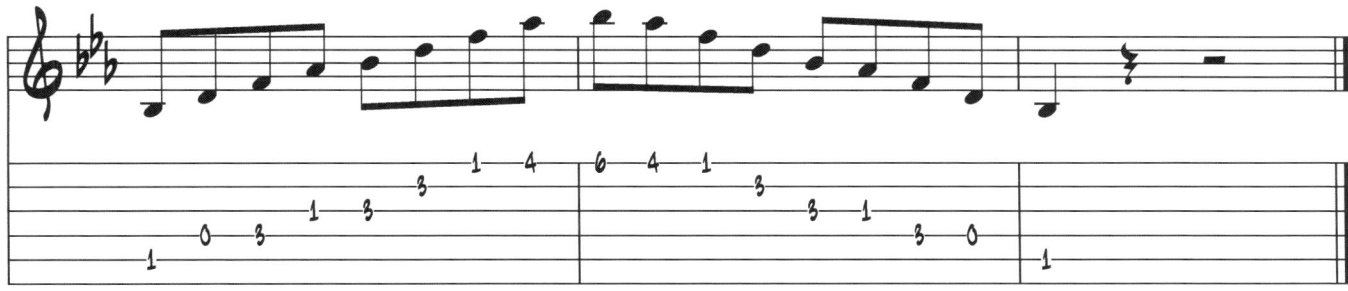

C Aeolian scale

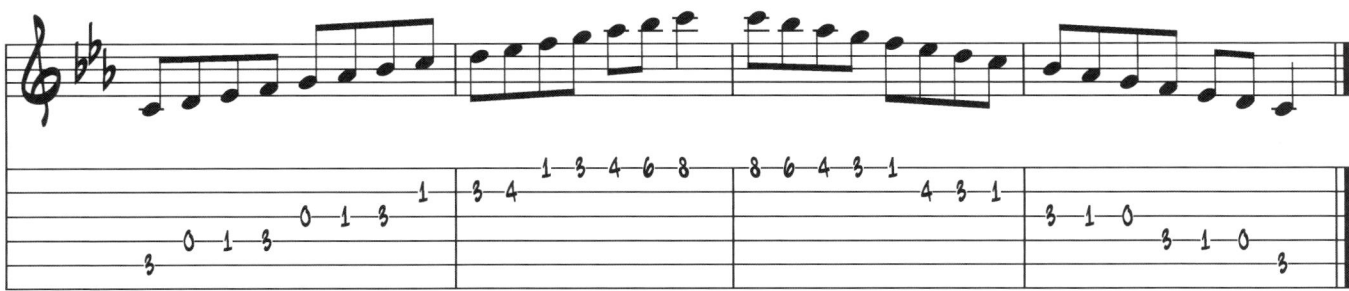

C min7 arpeggio

D Locrian scale

D min7 b5 arpeggio

4 Note Scale Groupings

The following exercise outlines the use of 4 note groupings moving stepwise diatonically through the scale of Eb major.

For example, the 4 note grouping starts on the root note or 1st degree of the scale and progresses stepwise. The exercise then descends from the 2nd octave Eb back to the root.

Ascending

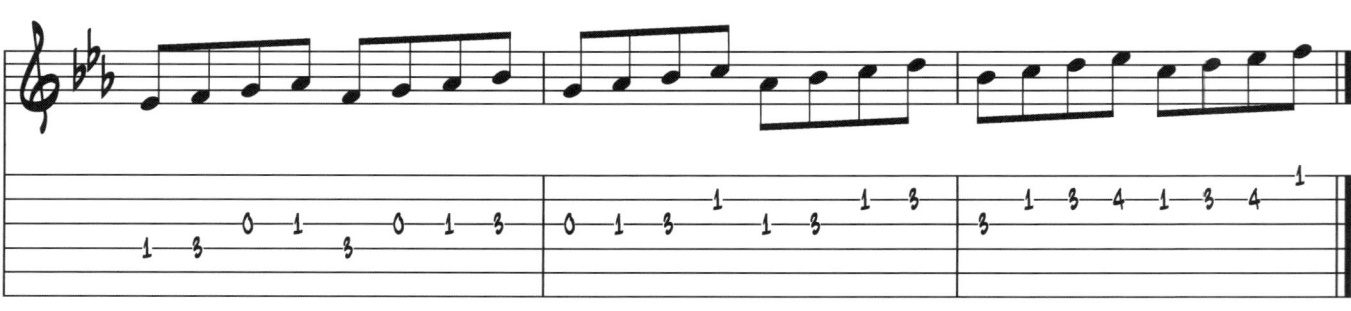

Descending

Permutation 2 — Up & Down

As in the previous exercise the following exercise outlines the use of 4 note groupings moving stepwise diatonically through the scale of Eb major.

Notice in exercise #2 the 4 note grouping starts on the root note or 1st degree of the scale and progresses stepwise. In this example we descend when we hit the 5th note in the sequence eg. descending from the 2nd 4 note grouping.

Ascending

Descending

Broken Thirds

Ascending

Descending

4 Note Groupings Diatonic Triads

4 Note Groupings Diatonic 7th Chords

Ascending

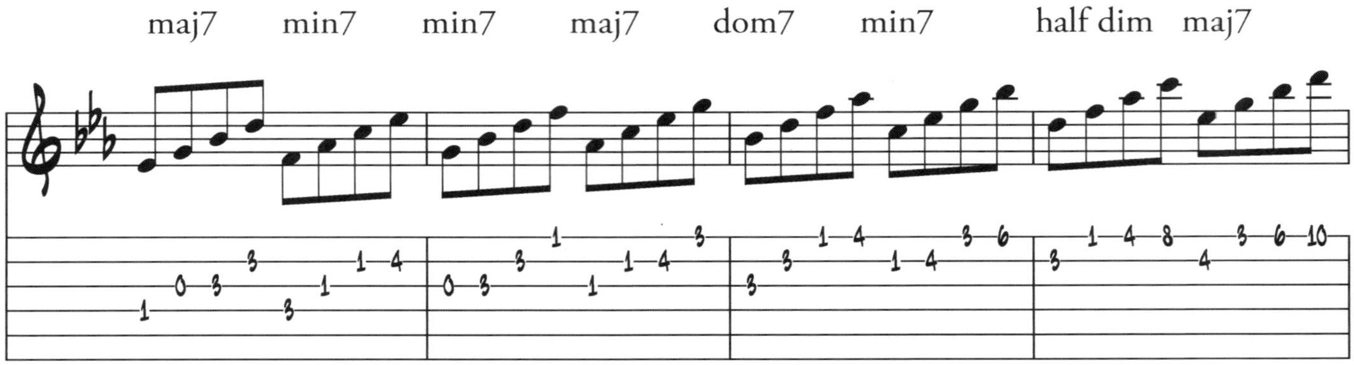

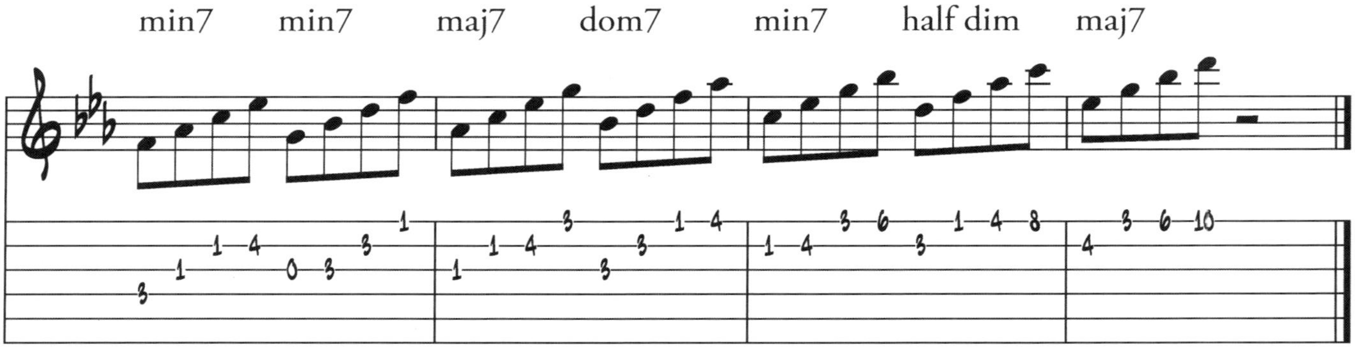

maj7   min7   min7   maj7   dom7   min7   half dim   maj7

min7   min7   maj7   dom7   min7   half dim   maj7

Descending

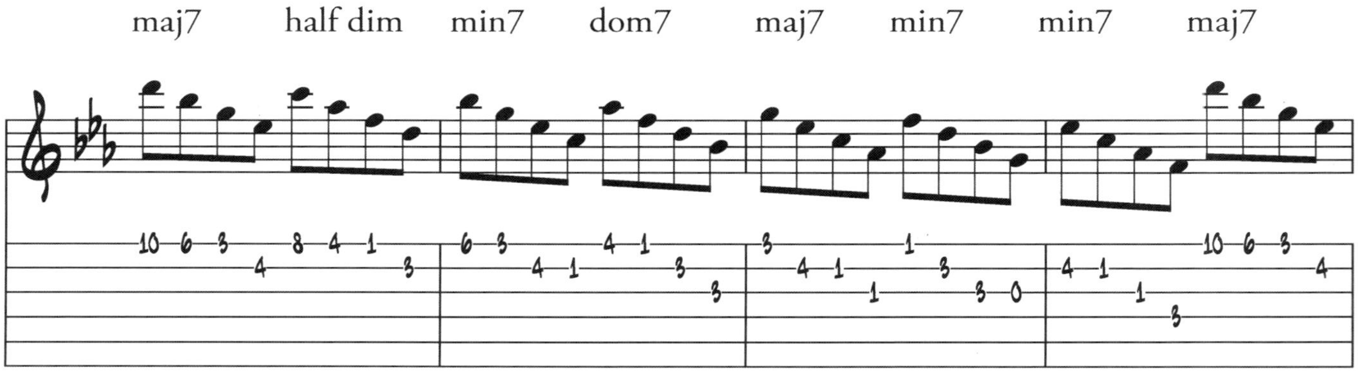

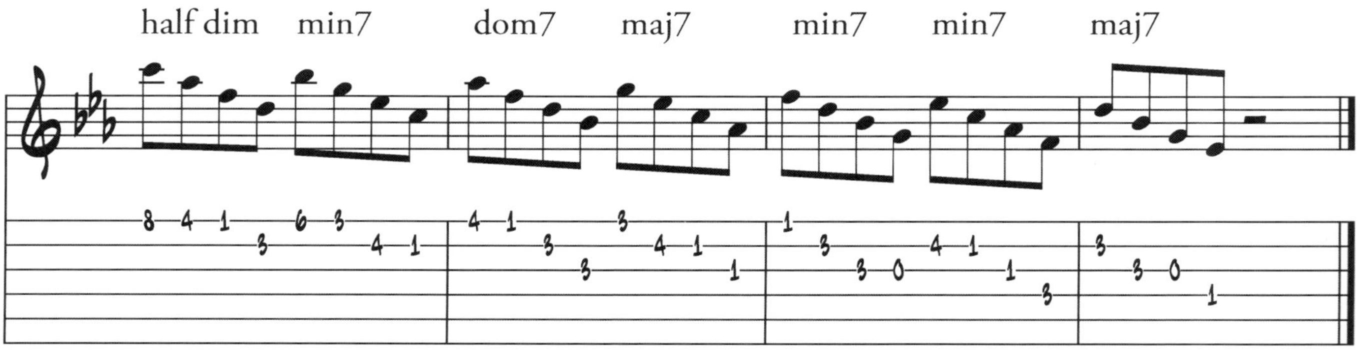

maj7   half dim   min7   dom7   maj7   min7   min7   maj7

half dim   min7   dom7   maj7   min7   min7   maj7

Permutation 2
Ascending & descending

3 Note Groupings

Eb major scale in triplet groupings
Ascending

Descending

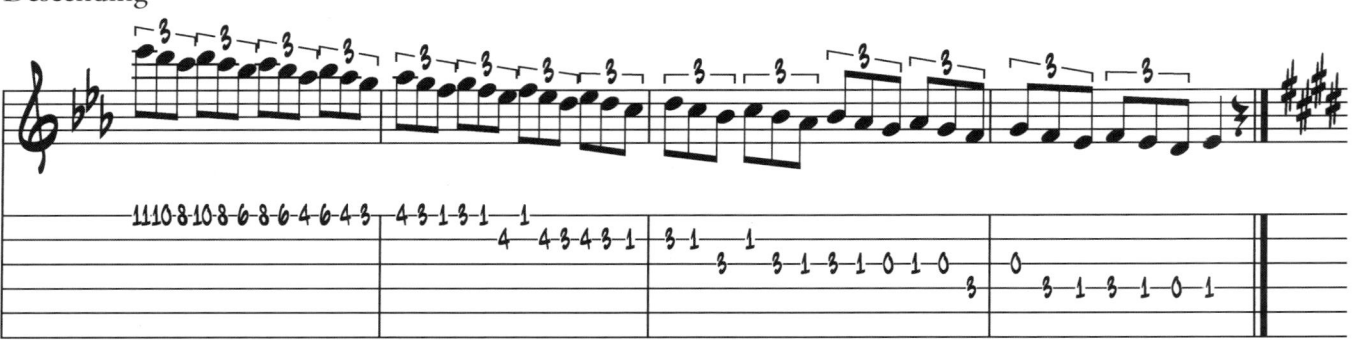

Scale studies in the key of E Major

Scales, Modes and Arpeggios over 2 octaves

E Major scale

E maj 7 arpeggio

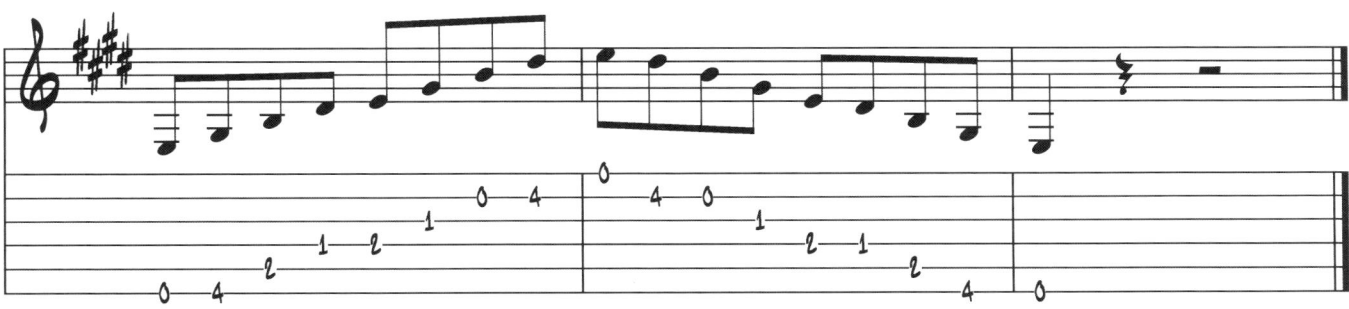

F# Dorian scale

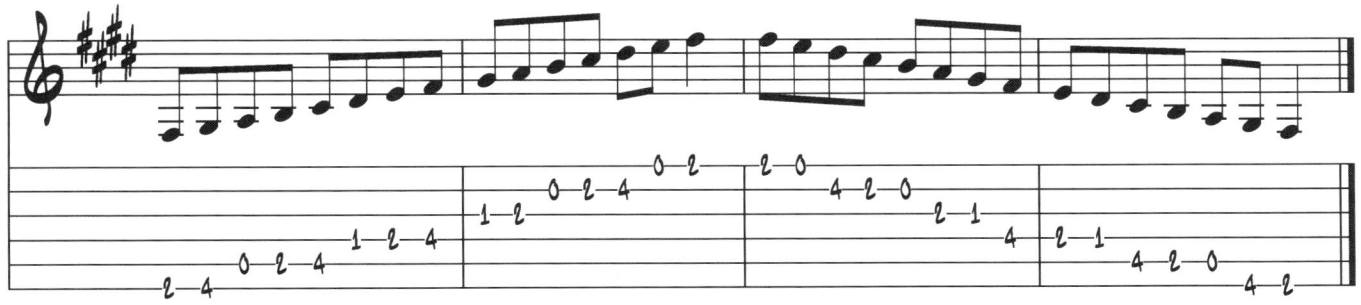

F# min 7 arpeggio

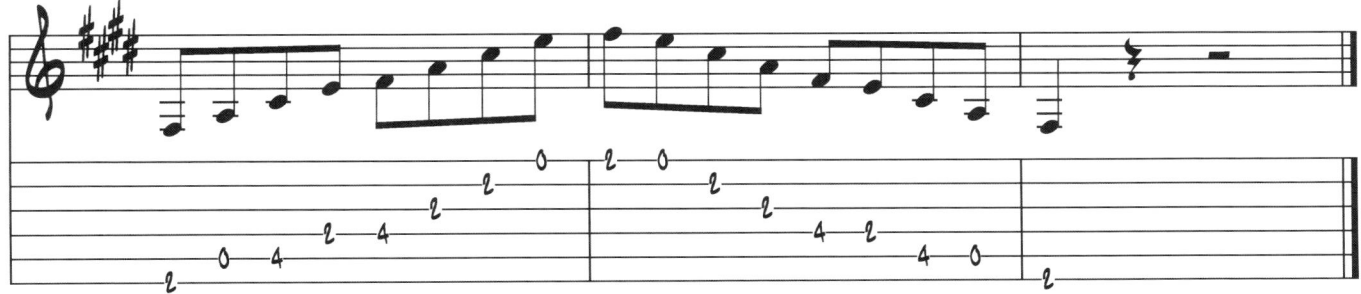

G# Phrygian scale

G# min 7 arpeggio

A Lydian scale

Amaj 7 arpeggio

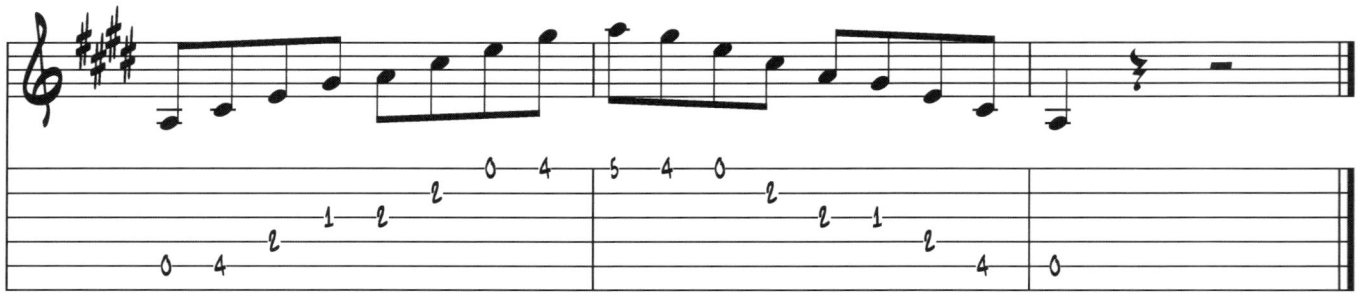

B Mixolydian scale

B 7 arpeggio

C# Aeolian scale

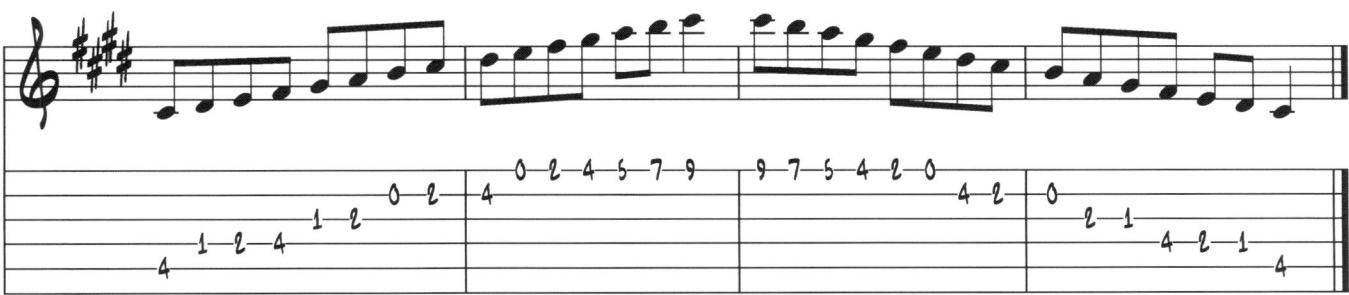

C# min7 arpeggio

D# Locrian scale

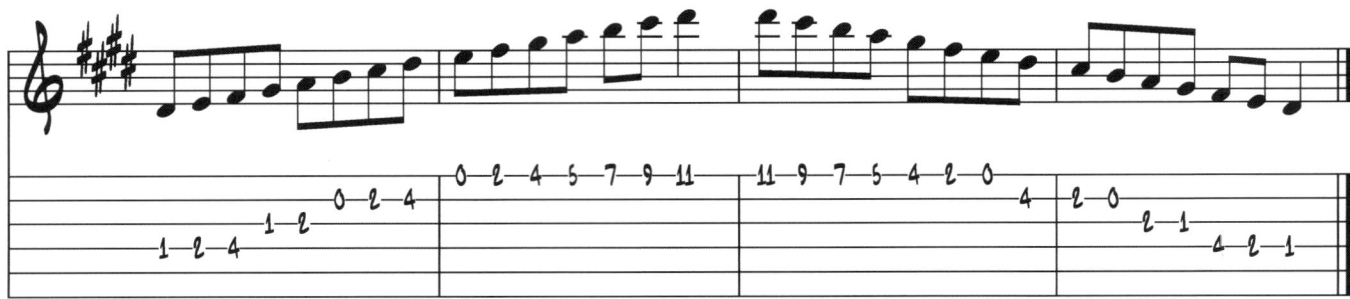

D# min7 b5 arpeggio

4 Note Scale Groupings

The following exercise outlines the use of 4 note groupings moving stepwise diatonically through the scale of E major.

For example, the 4 note grouping starts on the root note or 1st degree of the scale and progresses stepwise. The exercise then descends from the 2nd octave E back to the root.

Ascending

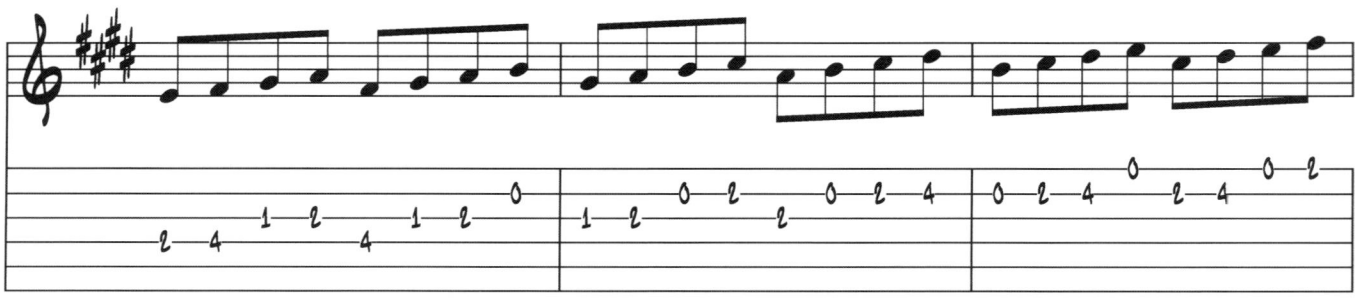

Descending

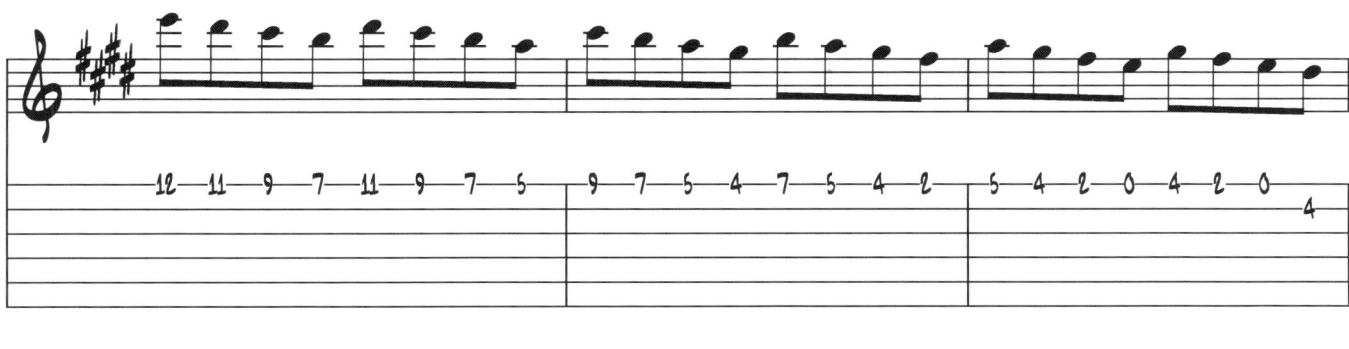

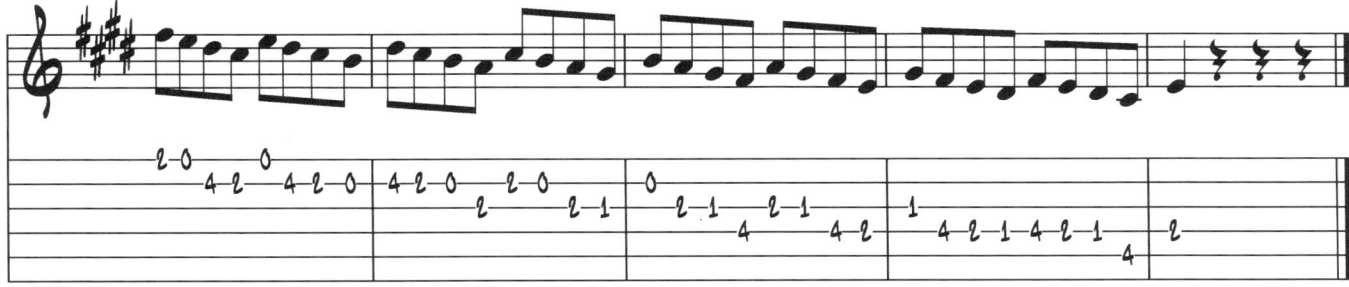

Permutation 2   Up & Down

As in the previous exercise the following exercise outlines the use of 4 note groupings moving stepwise diatonically through the scale of E major.

Notice in exercise #2 the 4 note grouping starts on the root note or 1st degree of the scale and progresses stepwise. In this example we descend when we hit the 5th note in the sequence eg. descending from the 2nd 4 note grouping.

Ascending

Descending

Broken Thirds

Ascending

Descending

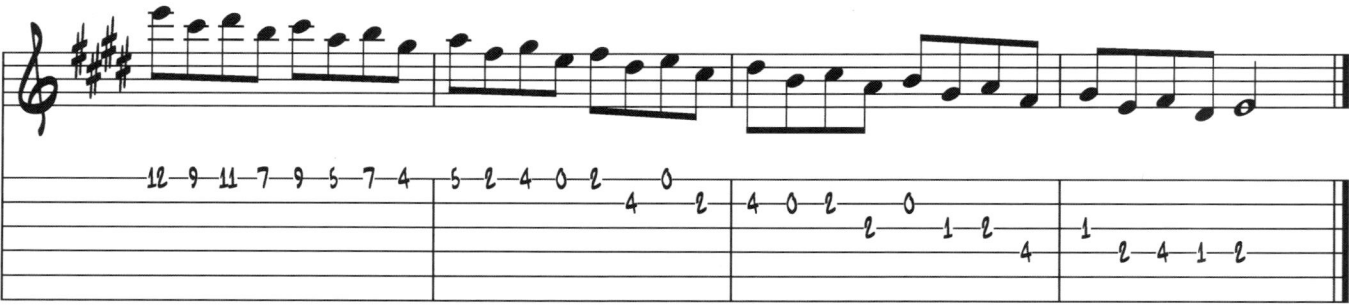

4 Note Groupings Diatonic Triads

4 Note Groupings Diatonic 7th Chords

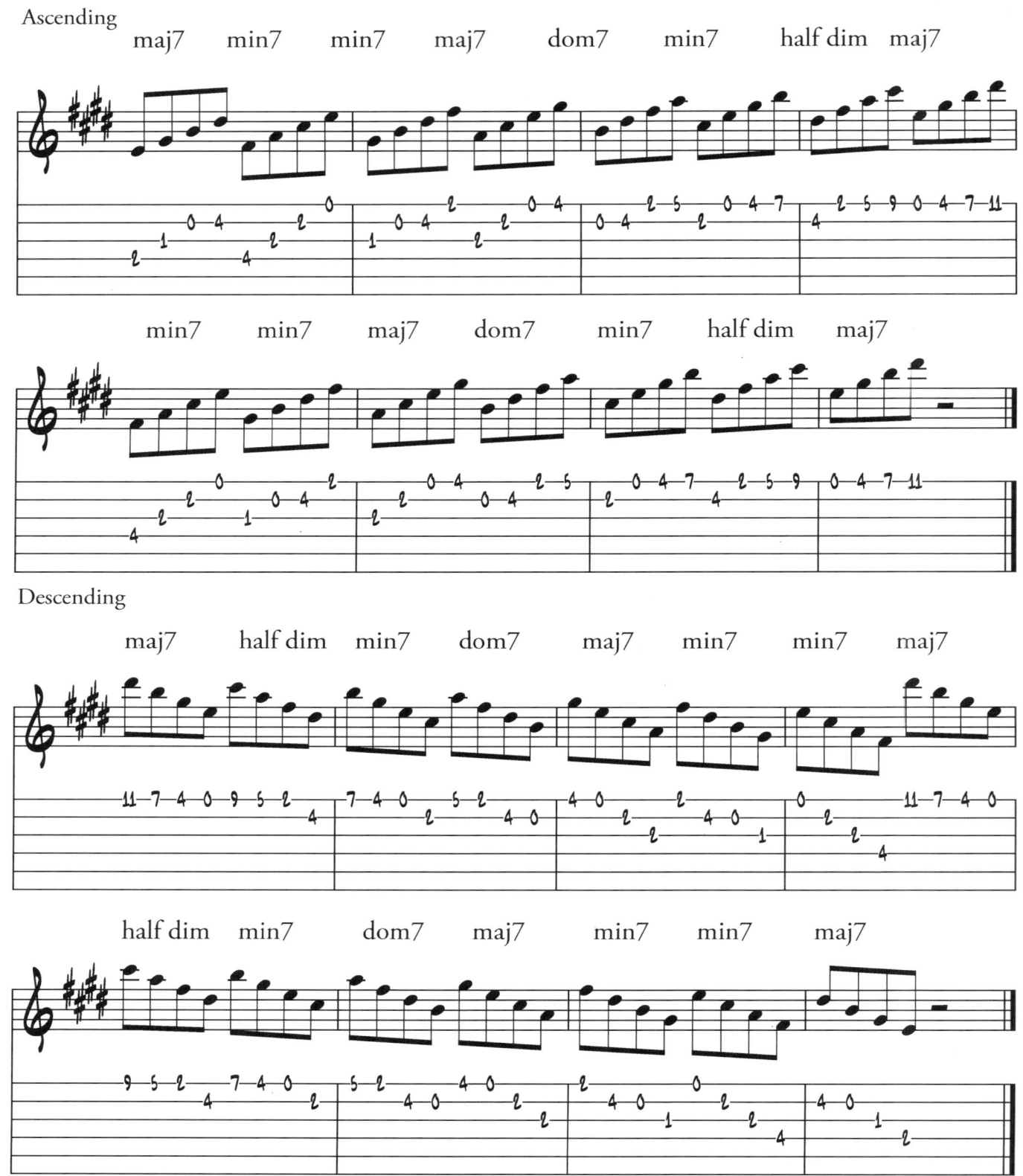

Ascending & descending

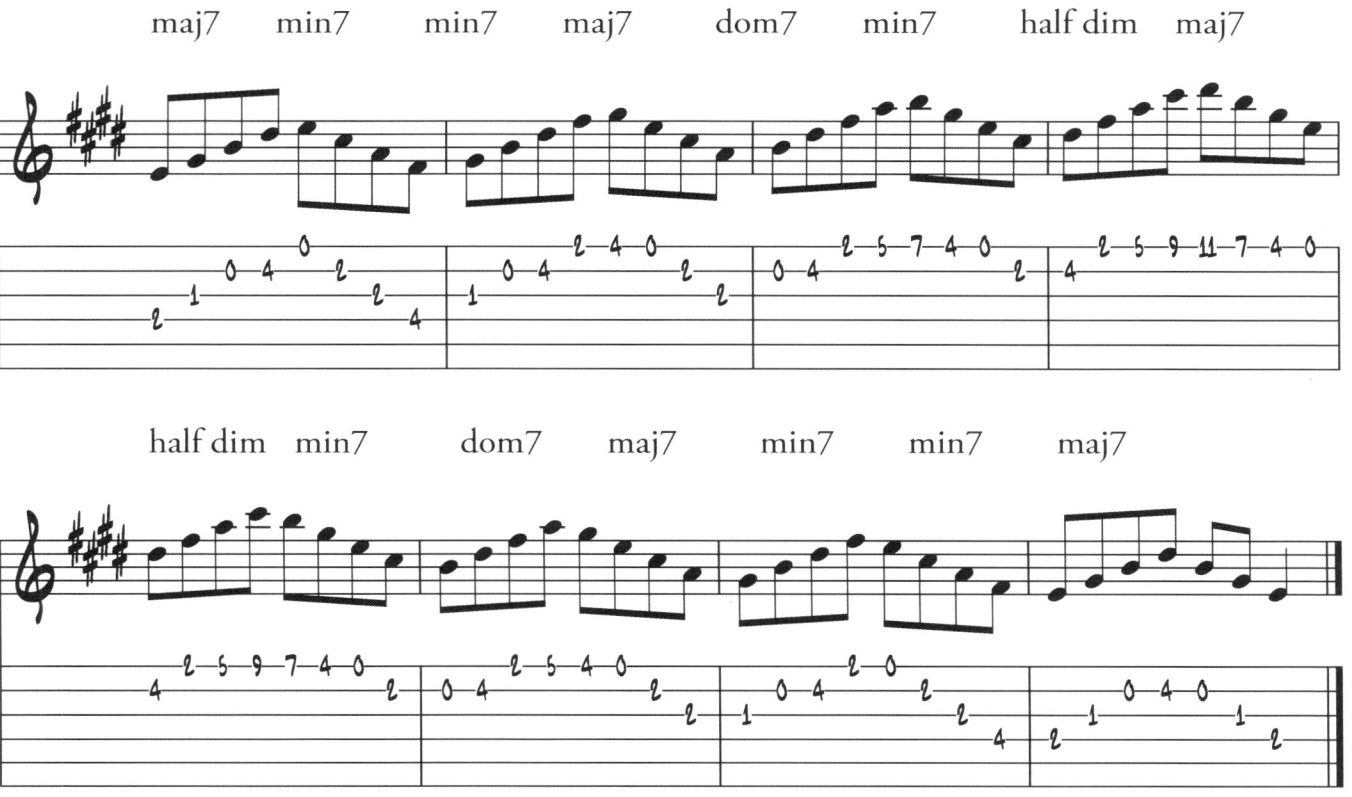

Permutation 3
Down the chord stepwise up the scale

3 Note Groupings

E major scale in triplet groupings
Ascending

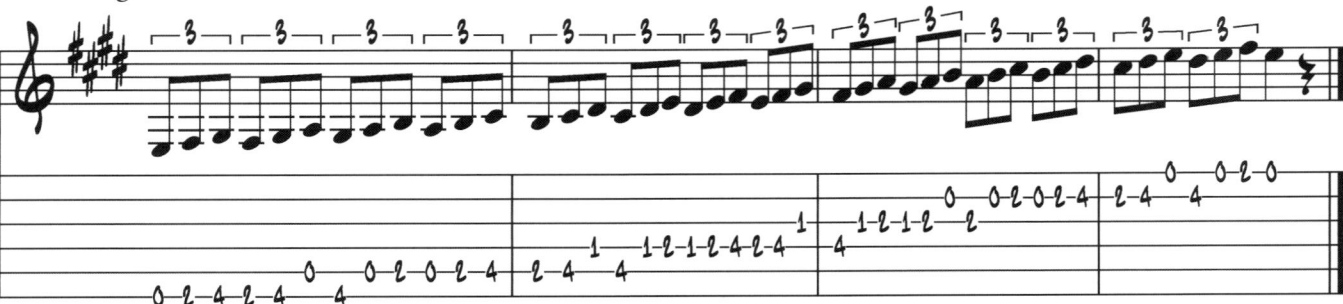

Descending

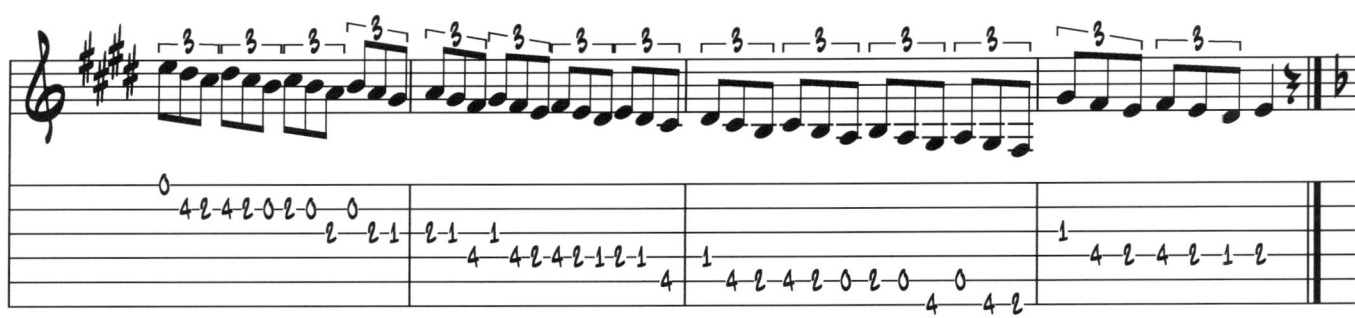

Scale studies in the key of F Major

Scales, Modes and Arpeggios over 2 octaves

F Major scale

F maj 7 arpeggio

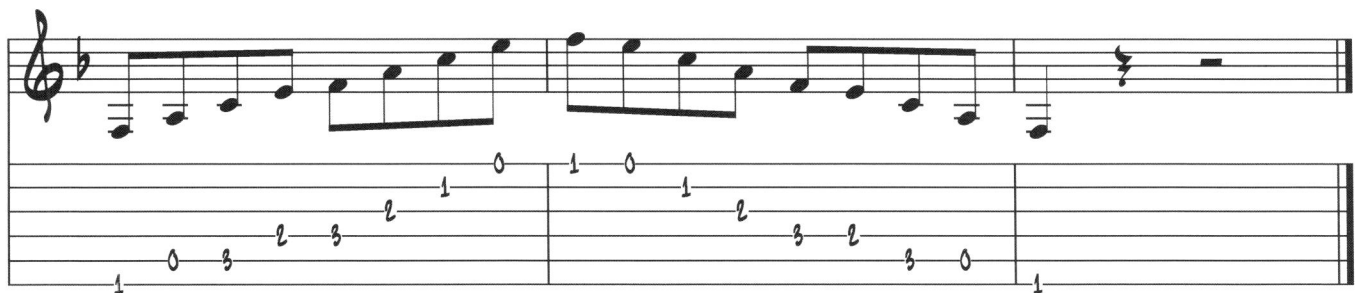

G Dorian scale

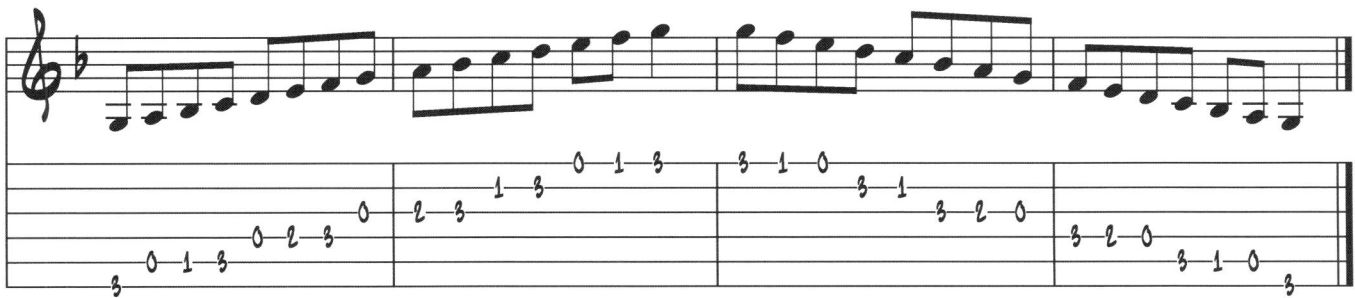

G min 7 arpeggio

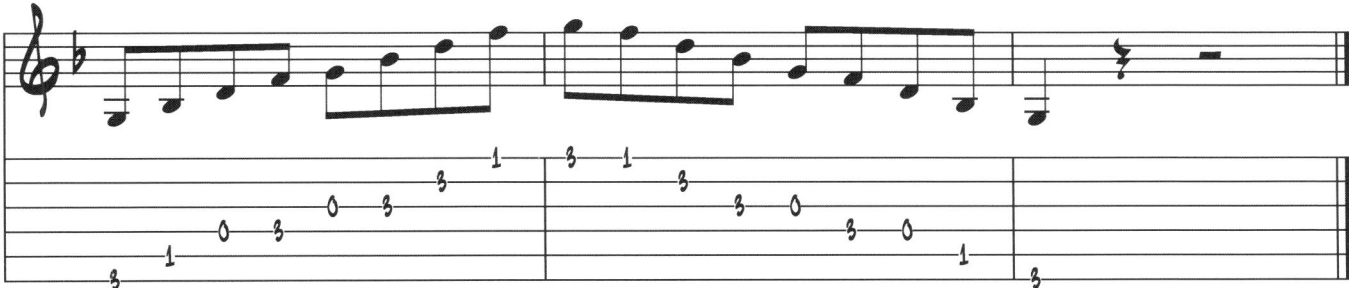

A Phrygian scale

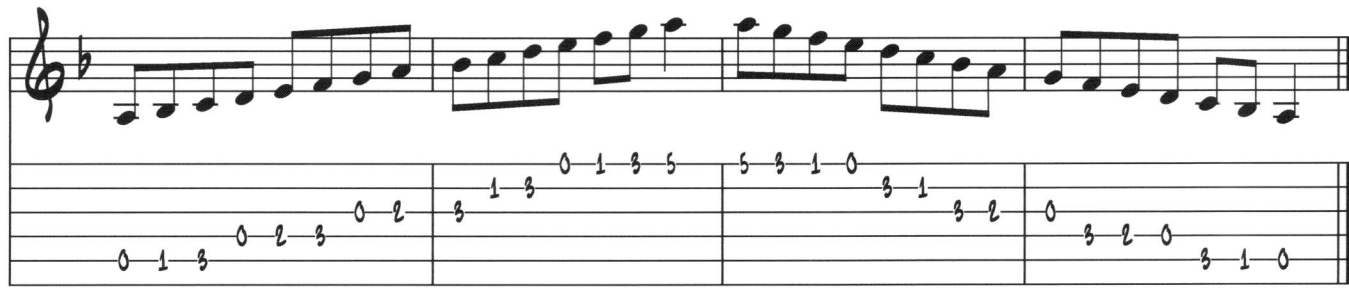

A min 7 arpeggio

Bb Lydian scale

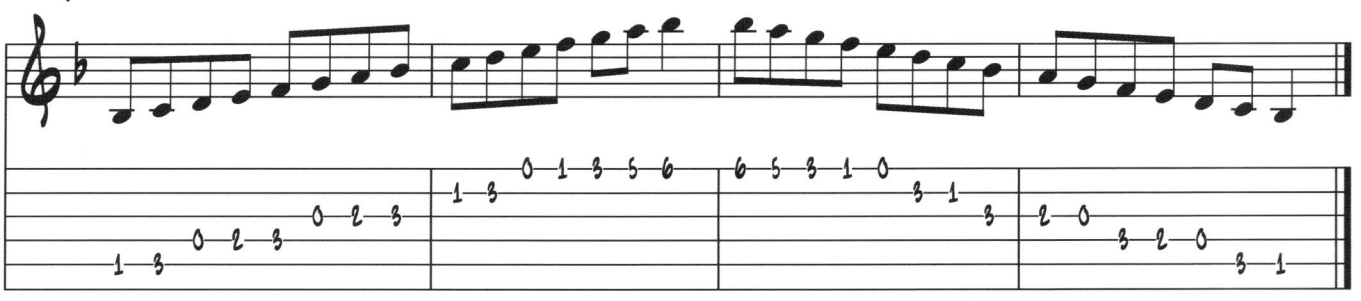

Bb maj 7 arpeggio

C Mixolydian scale

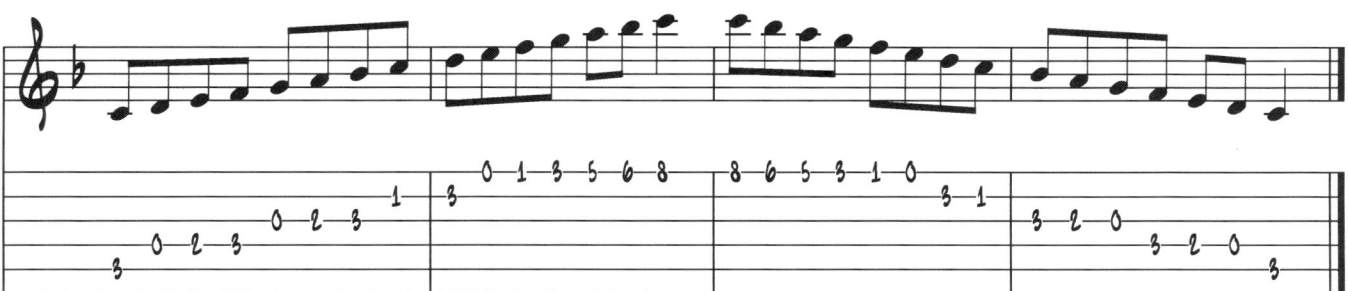

C 7 arpeggio

D Aeolian scale

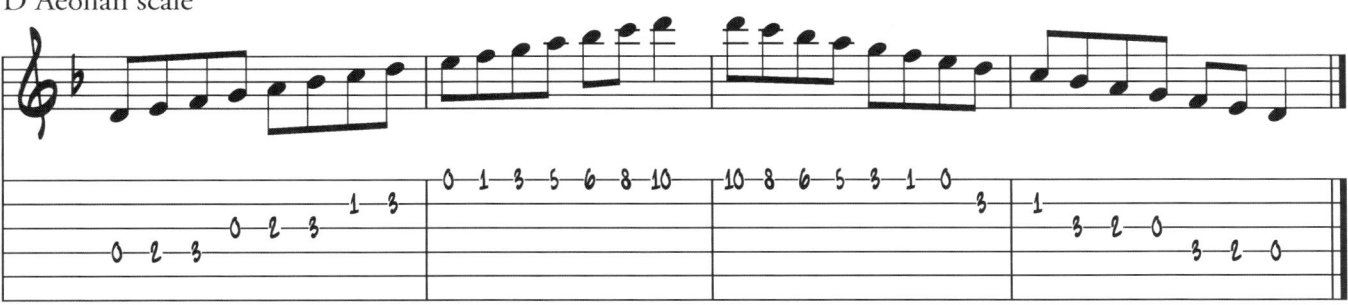

D min7 arpeggio

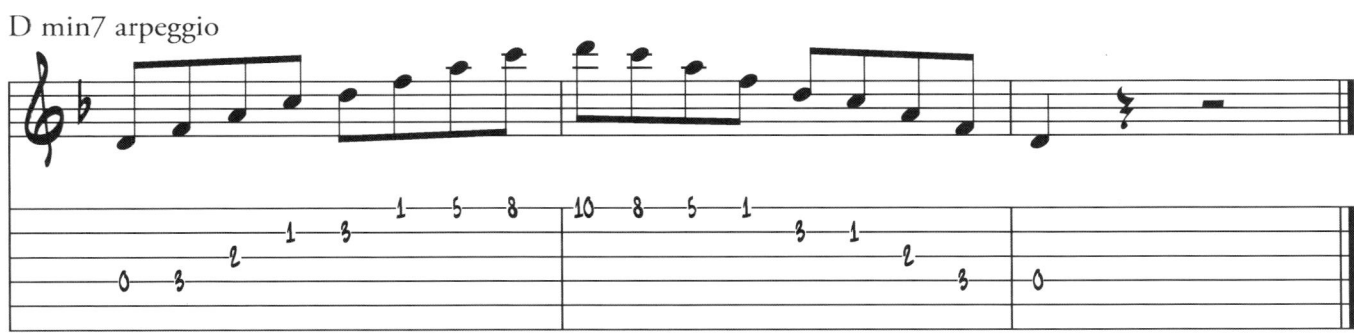

E Locrian scale

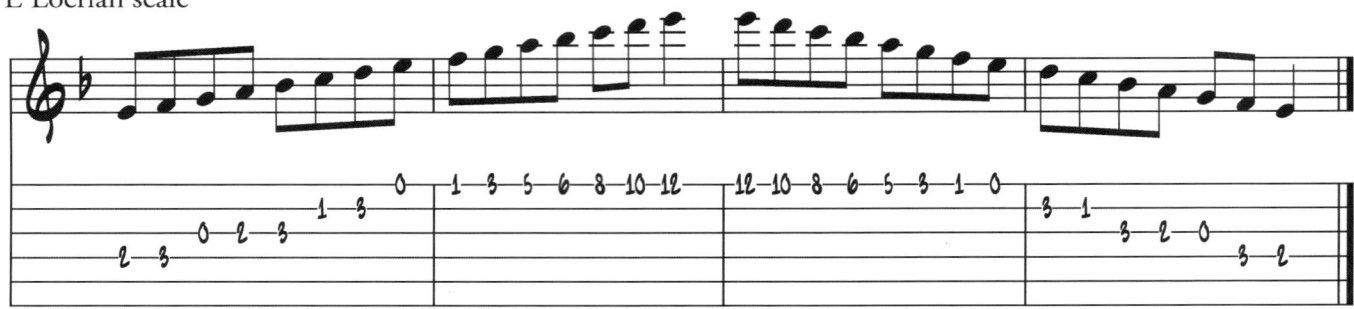

E min7 b5 arpeggio

4 Note Scale Groupings

The following exercise outlines the use of 4 note groupings moving stepwise diatonically through the scale of F major.

For example, the 4 note grouping starts on the root note or 1st degree of the scale and progresses stepwise. The exercise then descends from the 2nd octave F back to the root.

Ascending

Descending

Permutation 2   Up & Down

As in the previous exercise the following exercise outlines the use of 4 note groupings moving stepwise diatonically through the scale of F major.

Notice in exercise #2 the 4 note grouping starts on the root note or 1st degree of the scale and progresses stepwise. In this example we descend when we hit the 5th note in the sequence eg. descending from the 2nd 4 note grouping.

Ascending

Descending

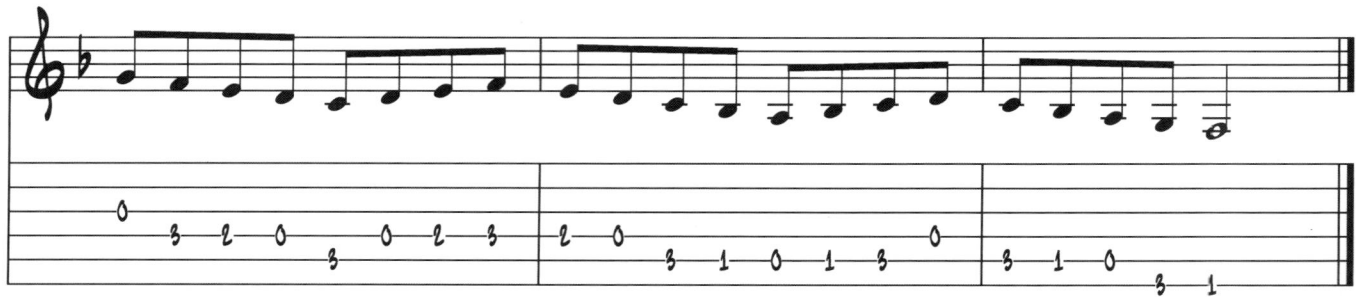

Broken Thirds

Ascending

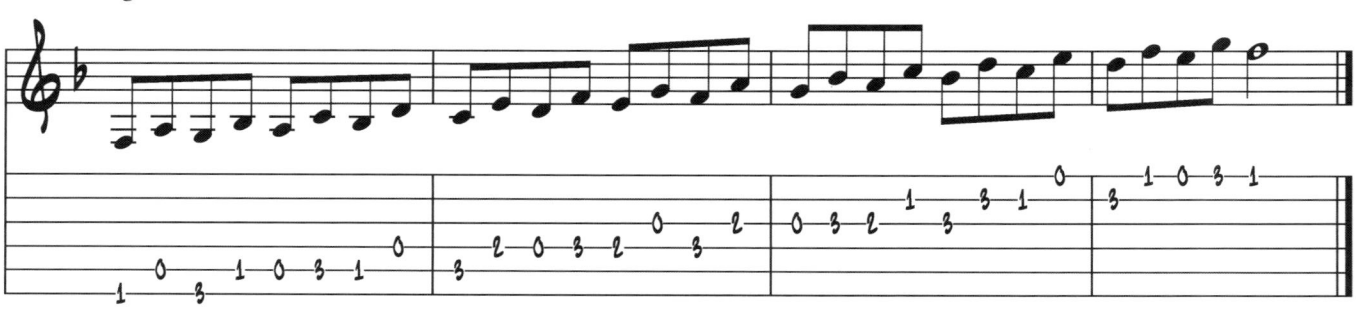

Descending

4 Note Groupings Diatonic Triads

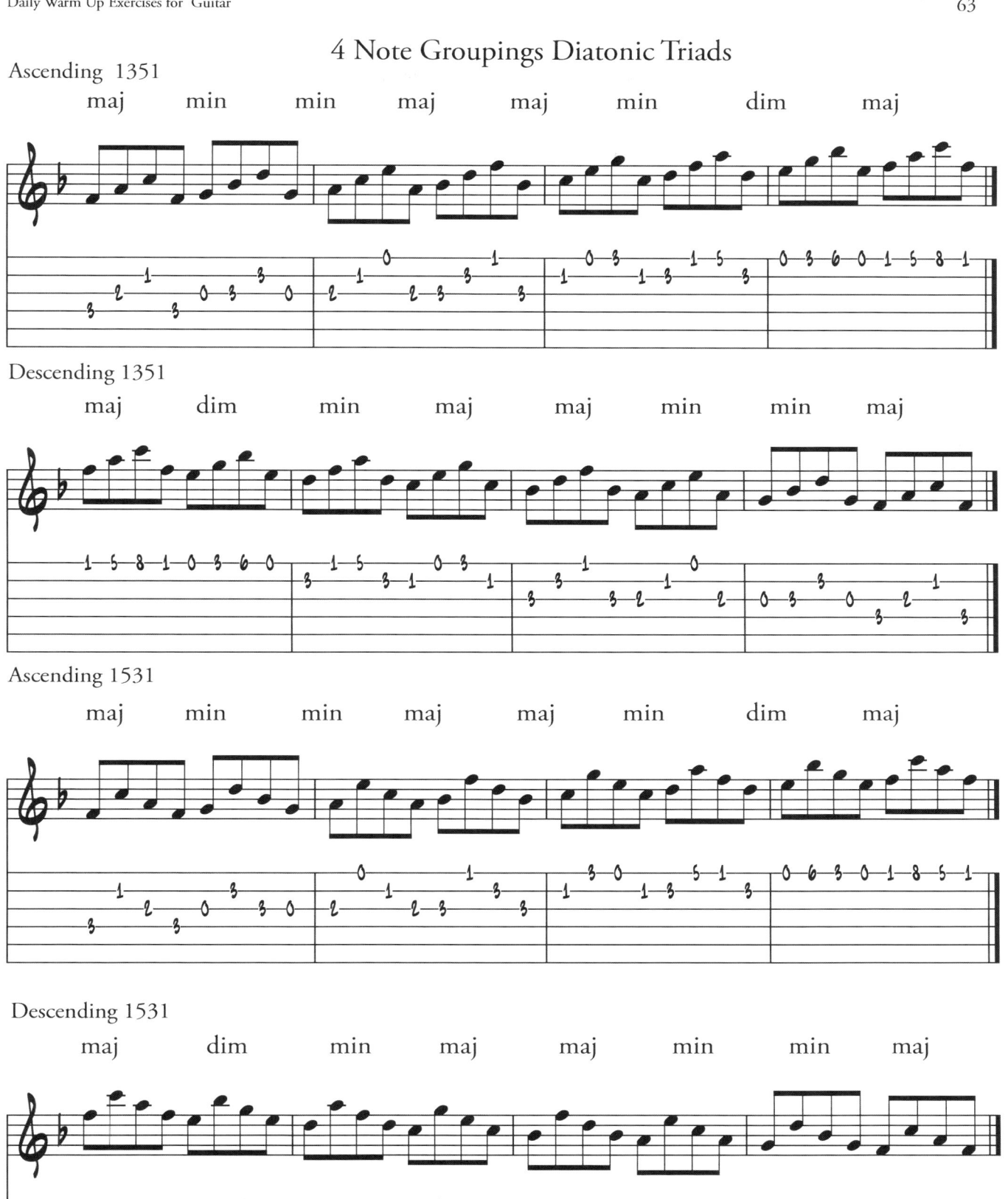

4 Note Groupings Diatonic 7th Chords

maj7   min7   min7   maj7   dom7   min7   half dim   maj7

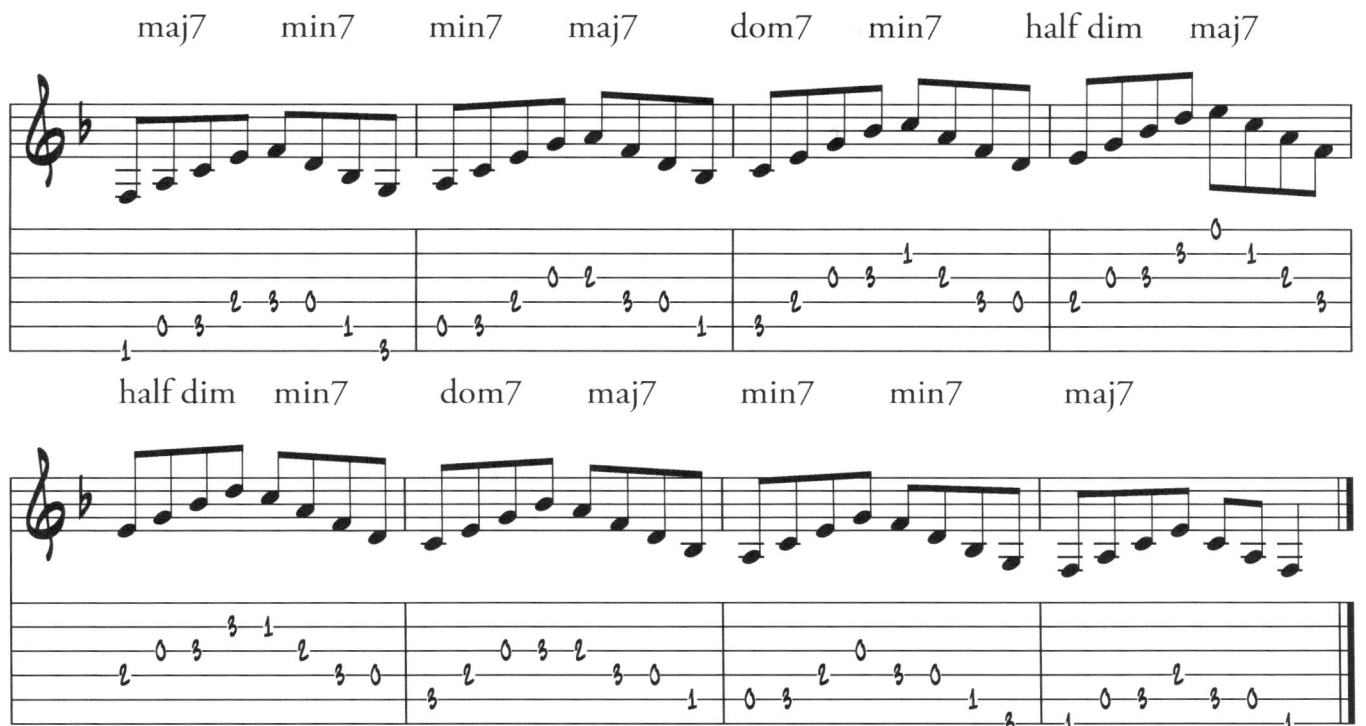

half dim   min7   dom7   maj7   min7   min7   maj7

Permutation 3
Down the chord stepwise up the scale

maj7   min7   min7   maj7   dom7   min7   half dim   maj7

maj7   half dim   min7   dom7   maj7   min7   min7   maj7

3 Note Groupings

F major scale in triplet groupings
Ascending

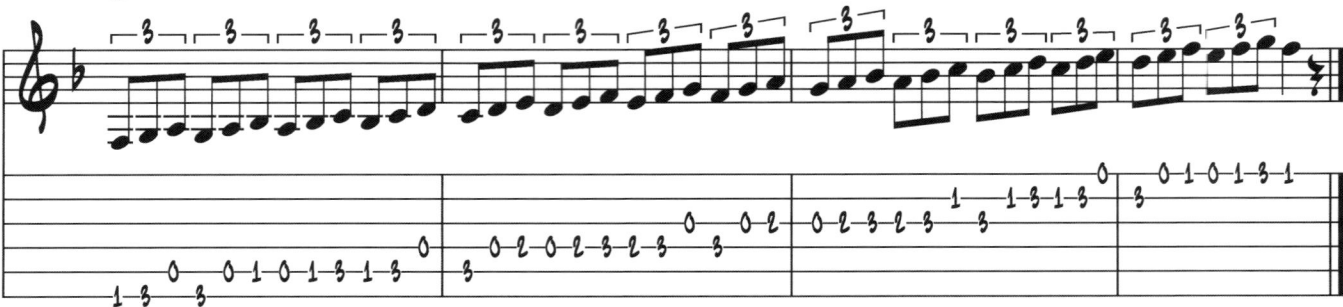

Descending

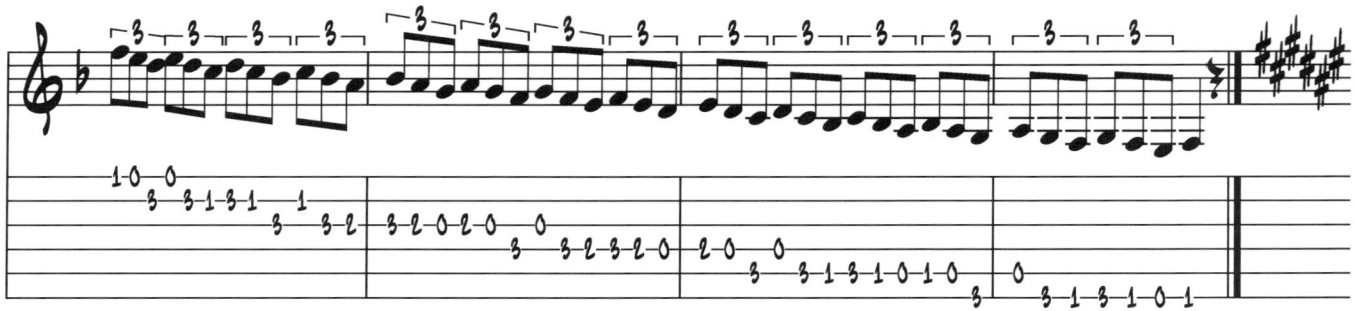

Scale studies in the key of F# Major

Scales, Modes and Arpeggios over 2 octaves

F# Major scale

F# maj 7 arpeggio

G# Dorian scale

G# min 7 arpeggio

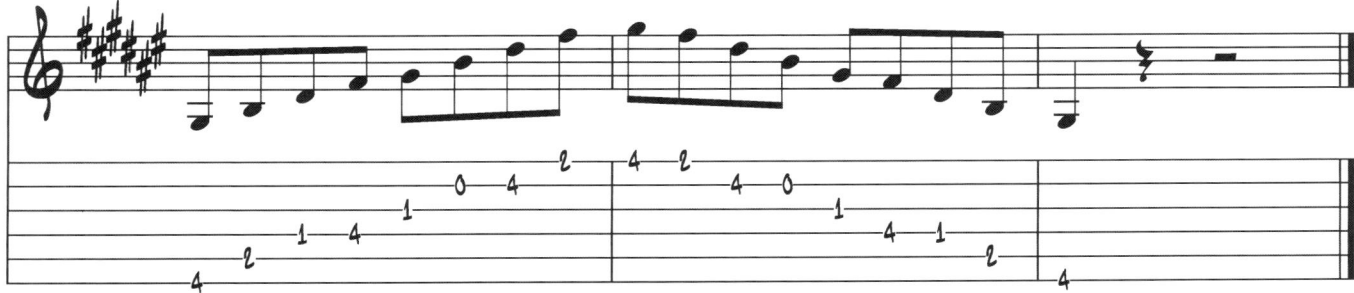

Daily Warm Up Exercises for Guitar

A# Phrygian scale

A# min 7 arpeggio

B Lydian scale

B major 7 arpeggio

C# Mixolydian scale

C# 7 arpeggio

D# Aeolian scale

D# min7 arpeggio

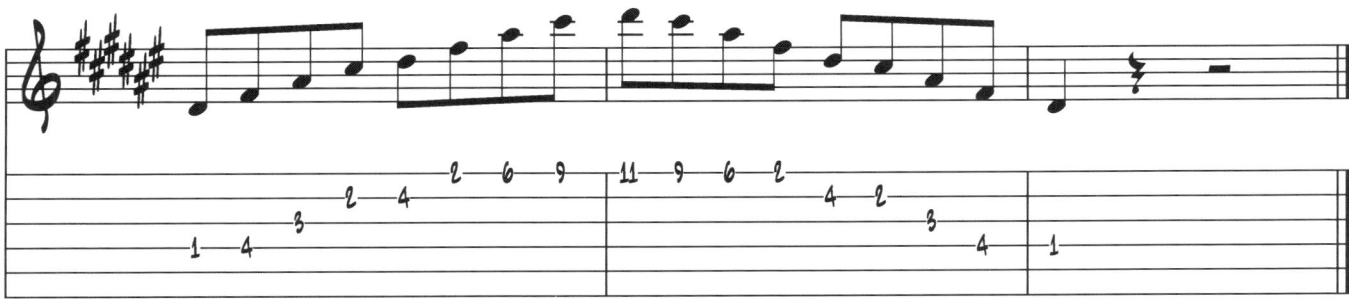

E# Locrian scale

E# min7 b5 arpeggio

4 Note Scale Groupings

The following exercise outlines the use of 4 note groupings moving stepwise diatonically through the scale of F# major.

For example, the 4 note grouping starts on the root note or 1st degree of the scale and progresses stepwise. The exercise then descends from the 2nd octave F# back to the root.

Ascending

Descending

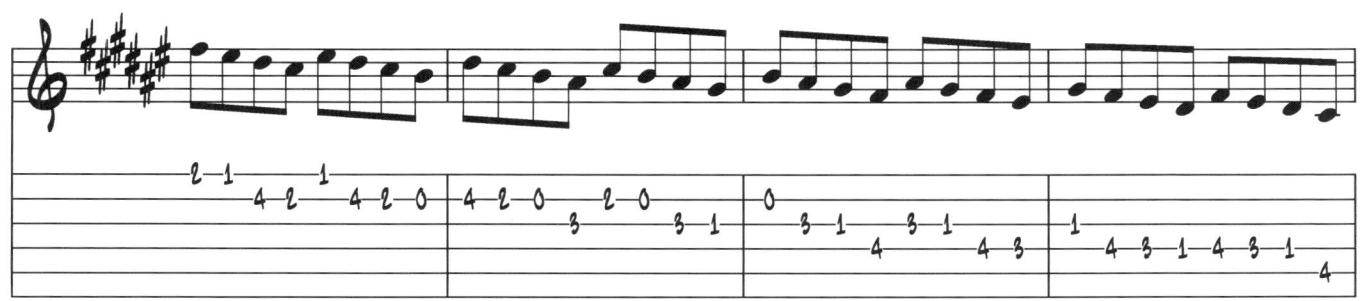

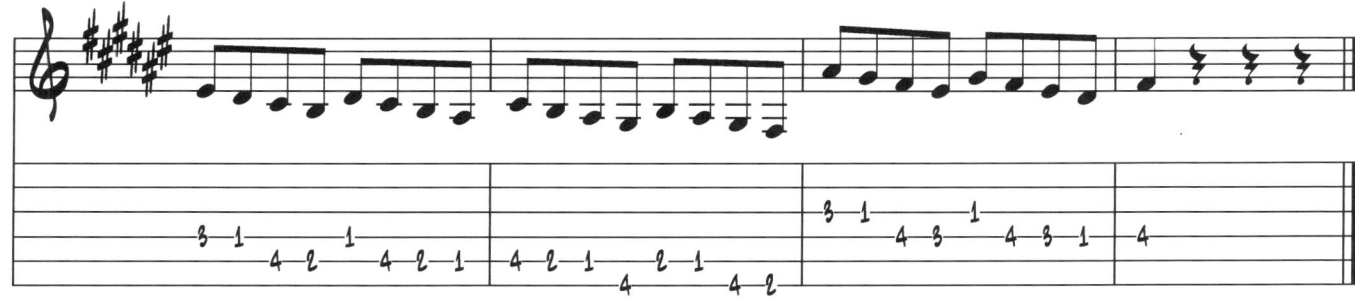

Permutation #2   Up & Down

As in the previous exercise the following exercise outlines the use of 4 note groupings moving stepwise diatonically through the scale of F# major.

Notice in exercise #2 the 4 note grouping starts on the root note or 1st degree of the scale and progresses stepwise. In this example we descend when we hit the 5th note in the sequence eg. descending from the 2nd 4 note grouping.

Ascending

Descending

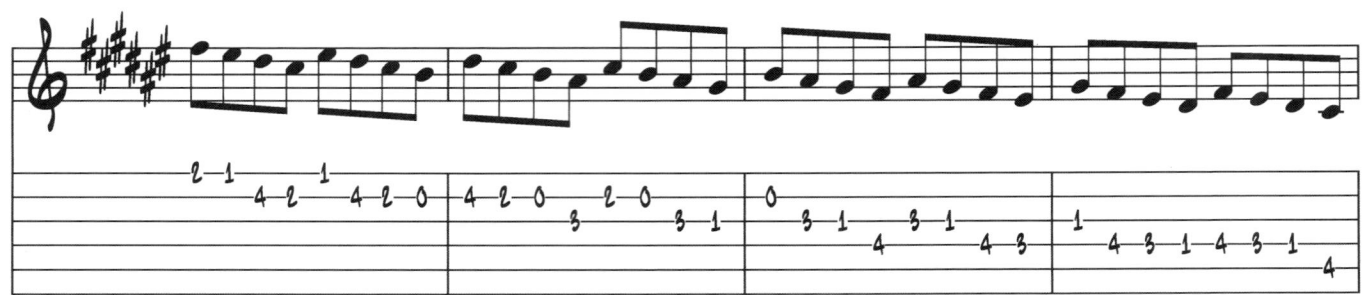

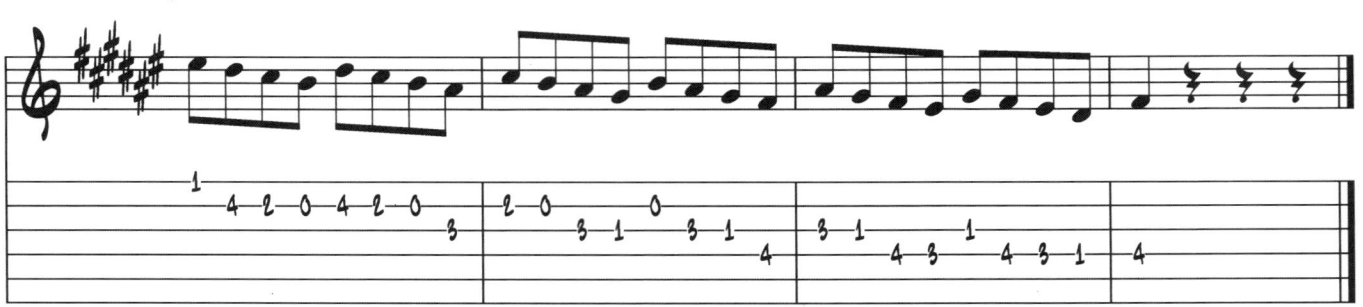

Broken Thirds

Ascending

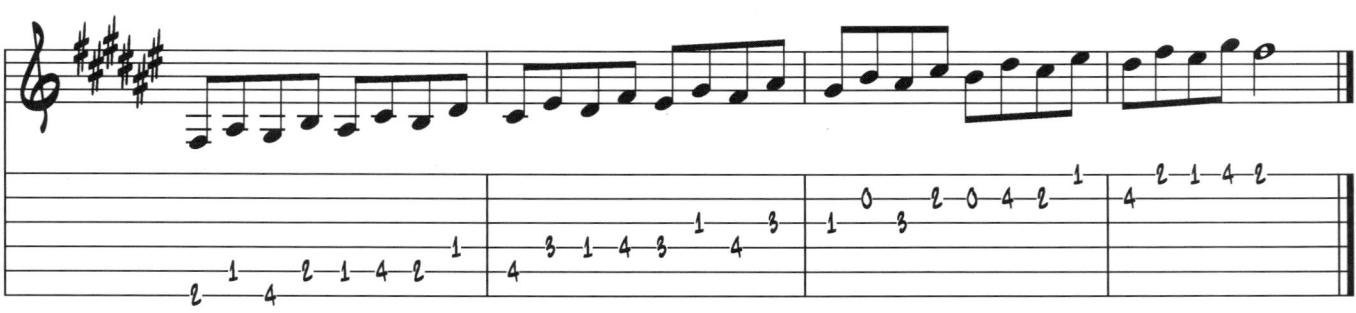

Descending

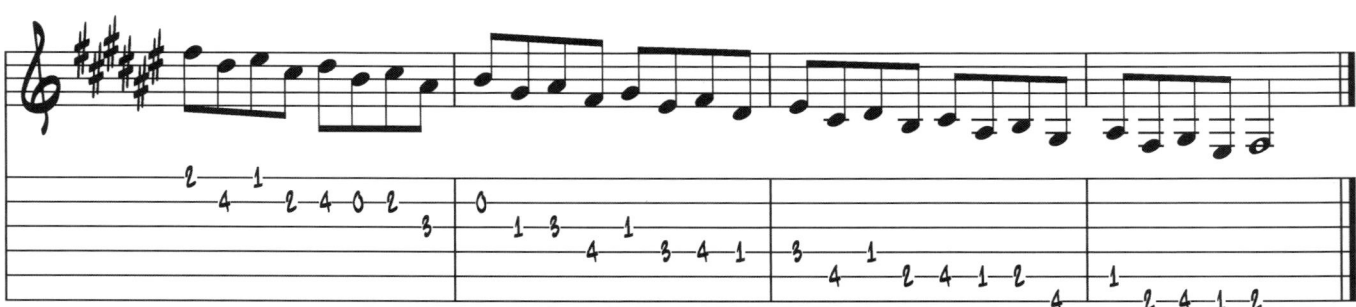

4 Note Groupings Diatonic Triads

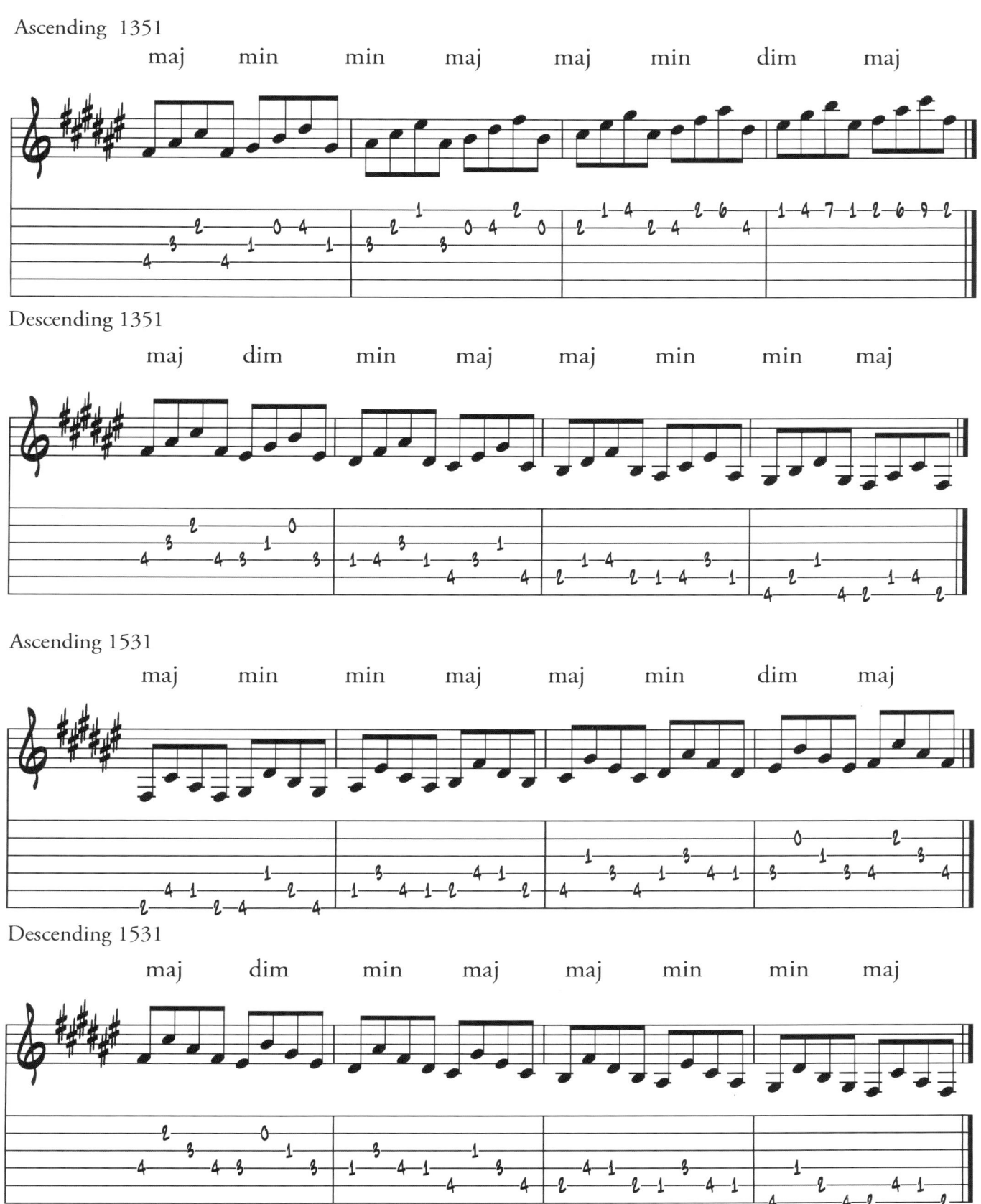

4 Note Groupings Diatonic 7th Chords

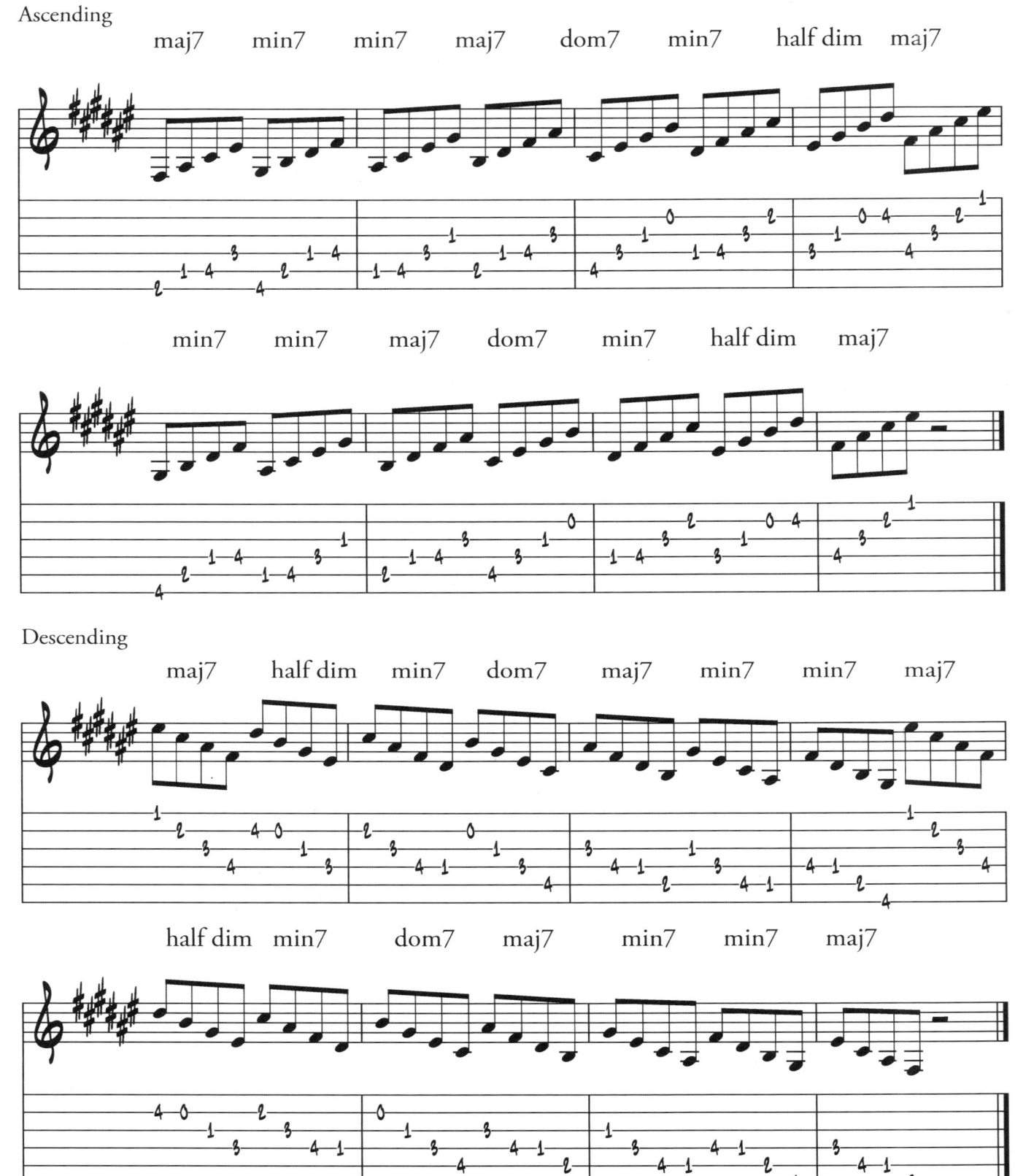

Permutation 2
Ascending & descending

maj7   min7   min7   maj7   dom7   min7   half dim maj7

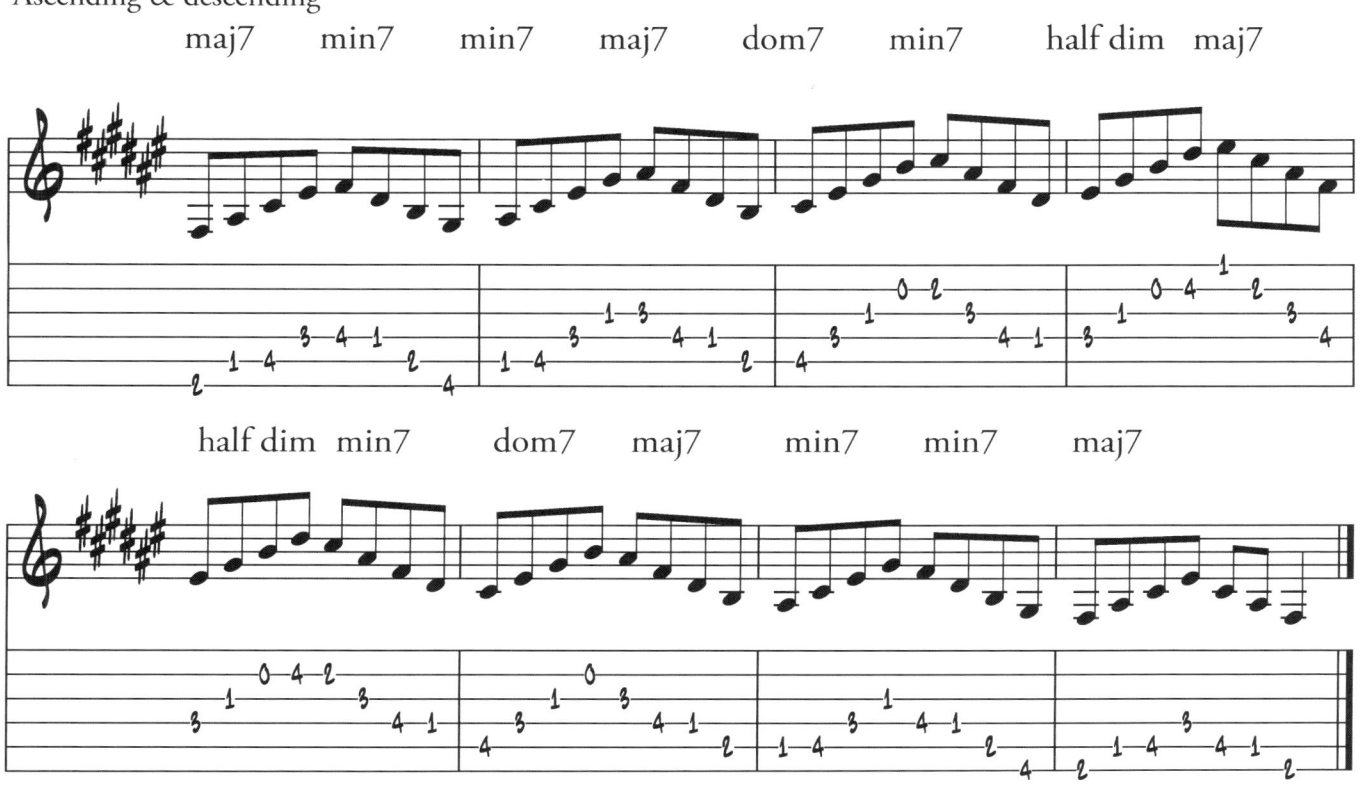

Permutation 3
Down the chord stepwise up the scale

maj7   min7   min7   maj7   dom7   min7   half dim maj7

3 Note Groupings

F# major scale in triplet groupings
Ascending

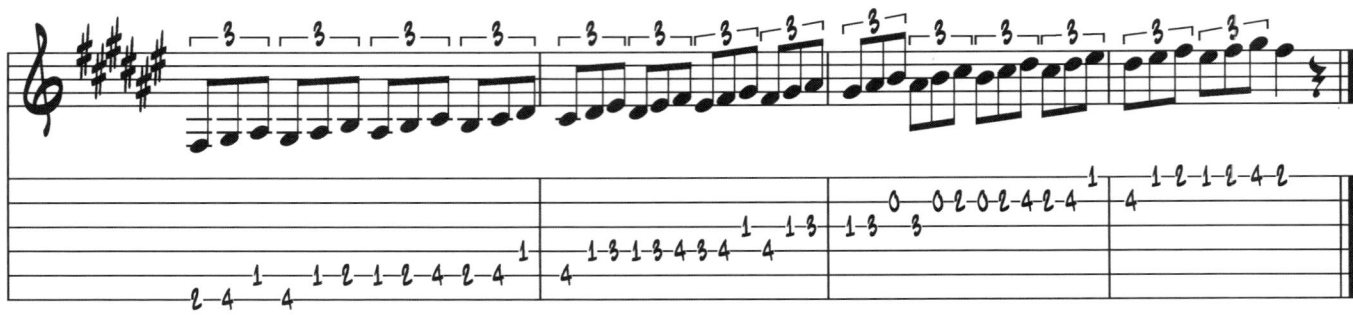

Descending

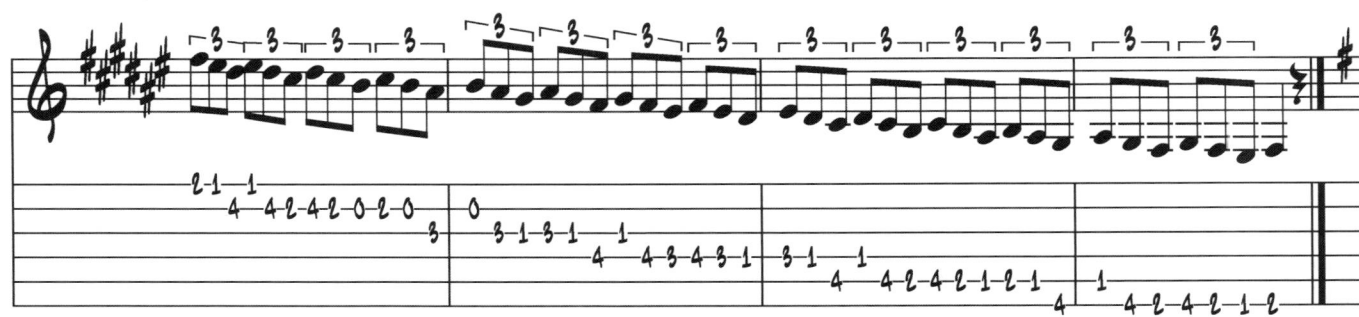

Scale studies in the key of G Major

Scales, Modes and Arpeggios over 2 octaves

G Major scale

G maj 7 arpeggio

A Dorian scale

A min 7 arpeggio

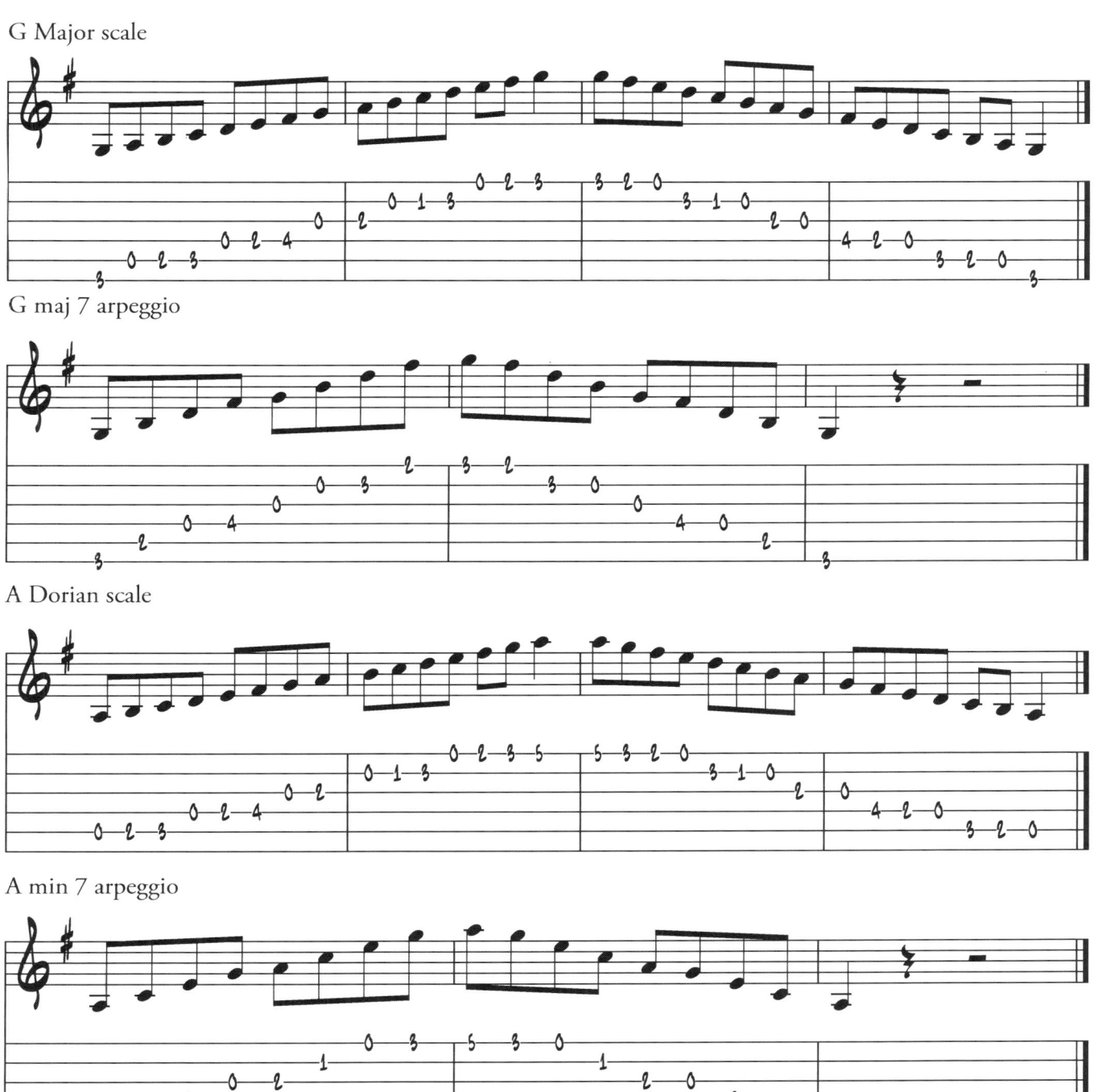

B Phrygian scale

B min 7 arpeggio

C Lydian scale

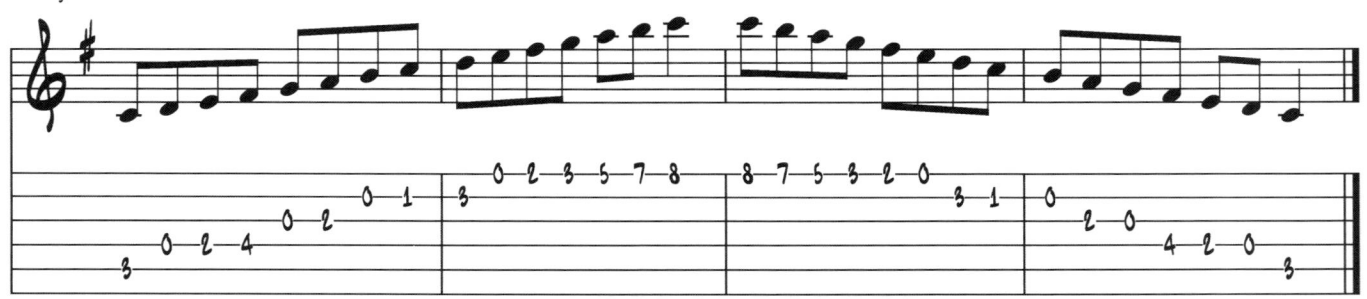

C maj 7 arpeggio

D Mixolydian scale

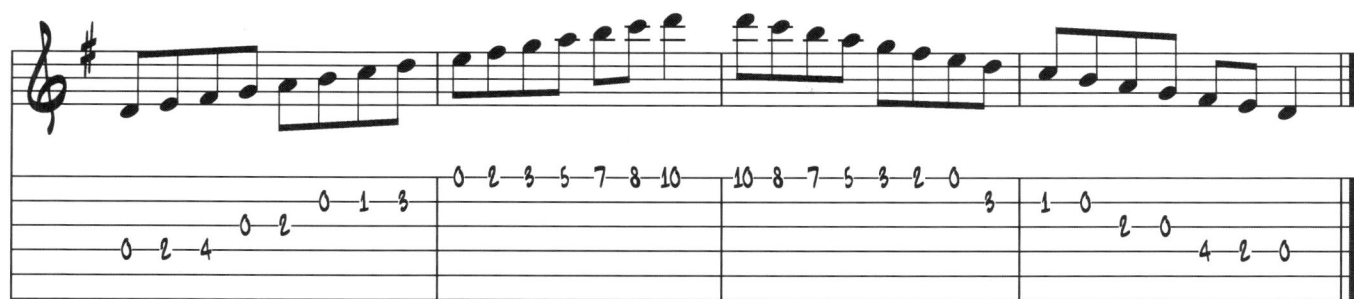

D 7 arpeggio

E Aeolian scale

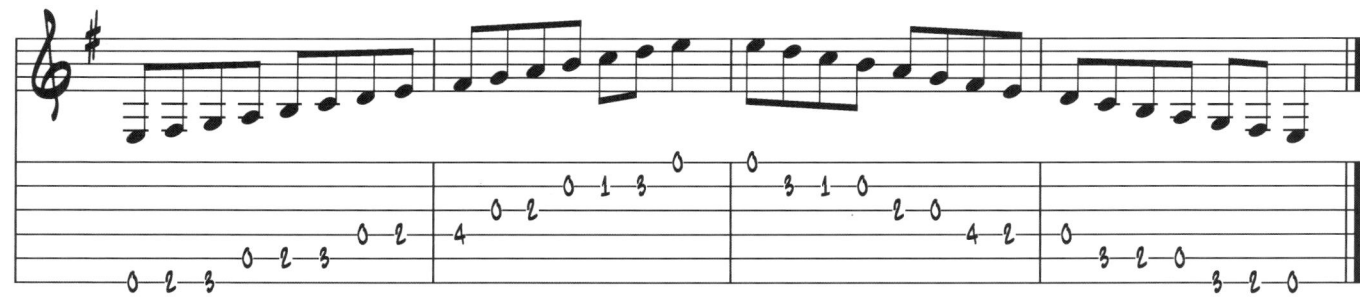

E min7 arpeggio

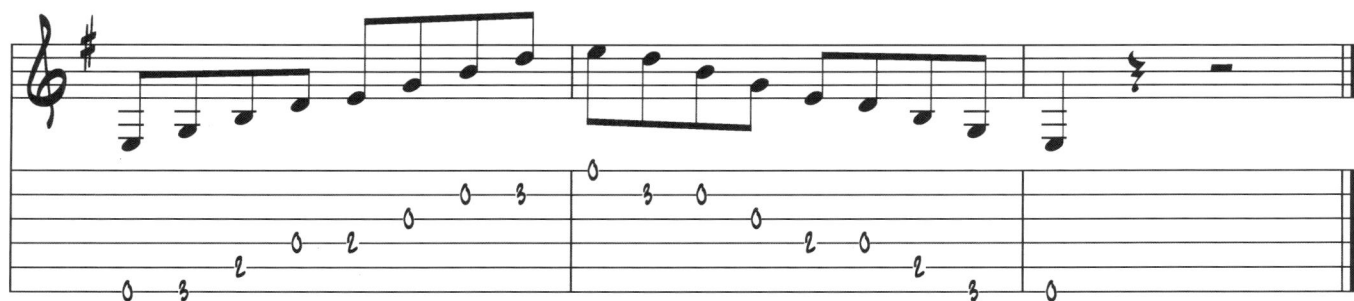

F# Locrian scale

F# min7 b5 arpeggio

4 Note Scale Groupings

The following exercise outlines the use of 4 note groupings moving stepwise diatonically through the scale of G major.

For example, the 4 note grouping starts on the root note or 1st degree of the scale and progresses stepwise. The exercise then descends from the 2nd octave G back to the root.

Ascending

Descending

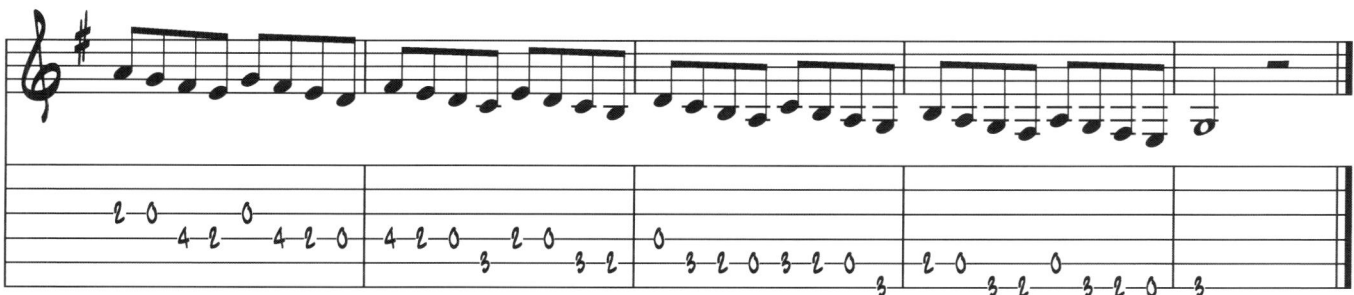

Permutation 2   Up & Down

As in the previous exercise the following exercise outlines the use of 4 note groupings moving stepwise diatonically through the scale of G major.

Notice in exercise #2 the 4 note grouping starts on the root note or 1st degree of the scale and progresses stepwise. In this example we descend when we hit the 5th note in the sequence eg. descending from the 2nd 4 note grouping.

Ascending

Descending

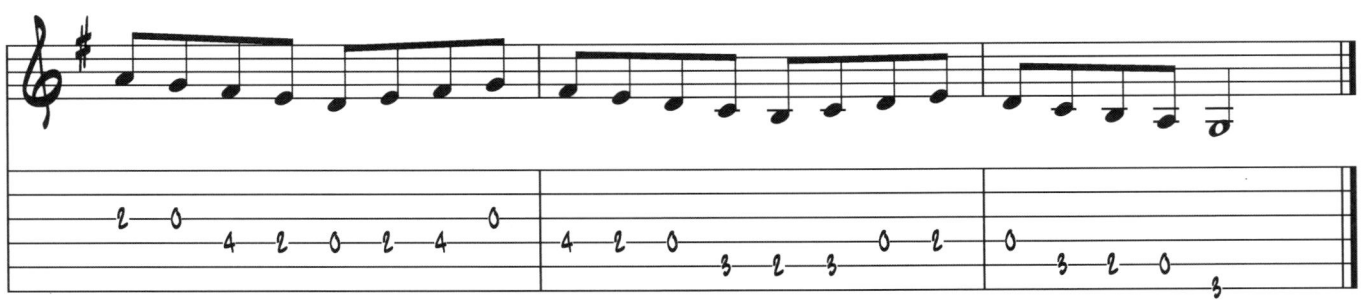

Broken Thirds

Ascending

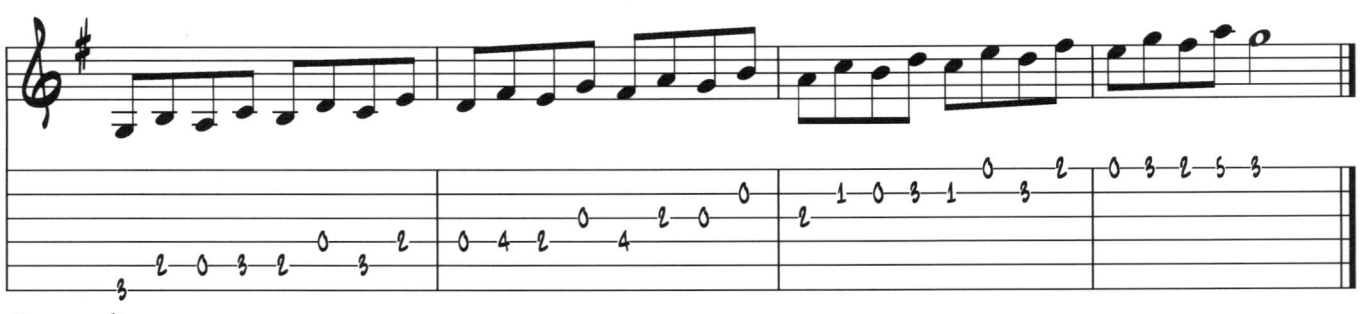

Descending

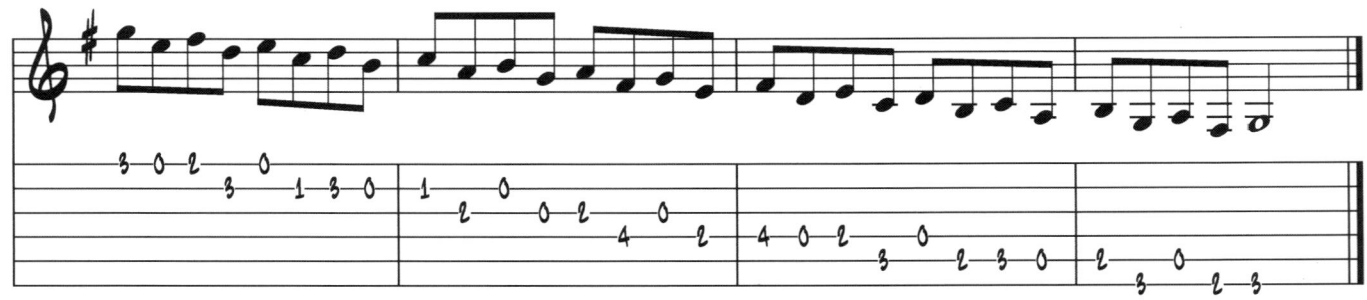

4 Note Groupings Diatonic Triads

Ascending 1351

4 Note Groupings Diatonic 7th Chords

Ascending

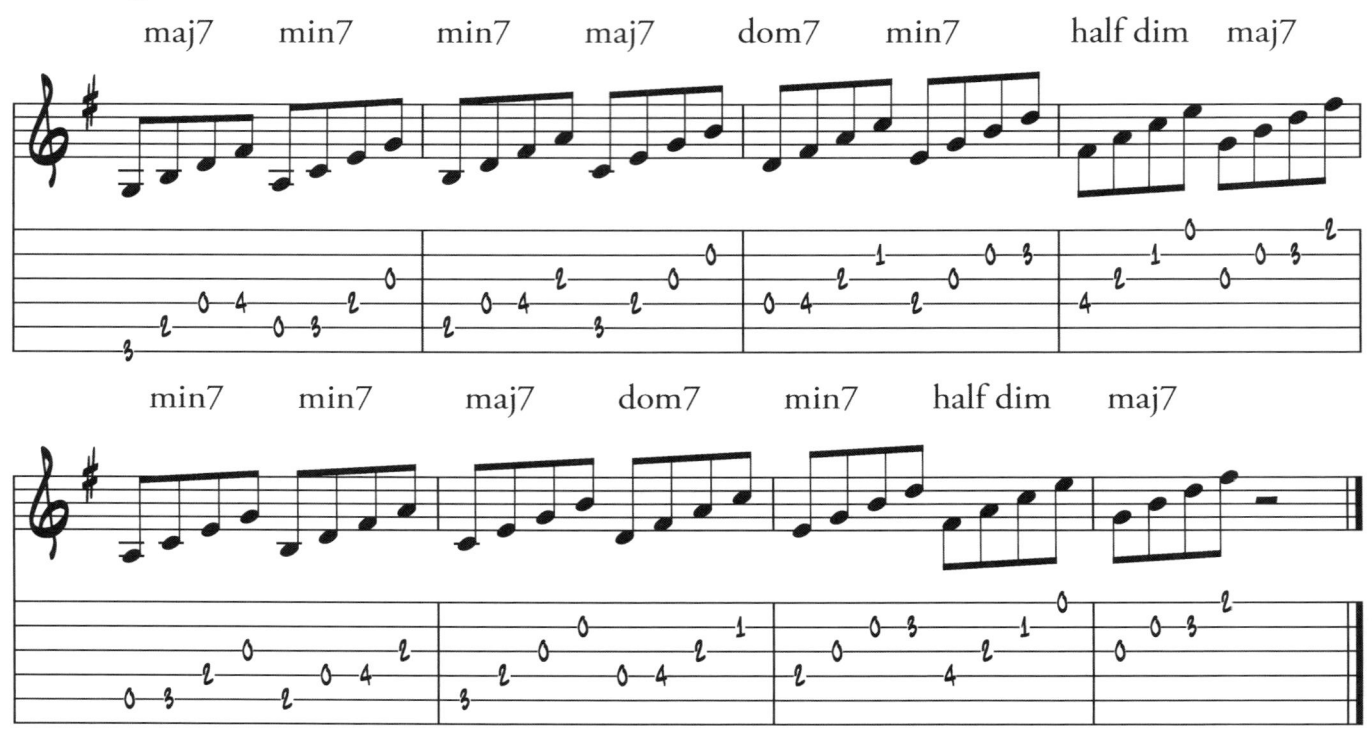

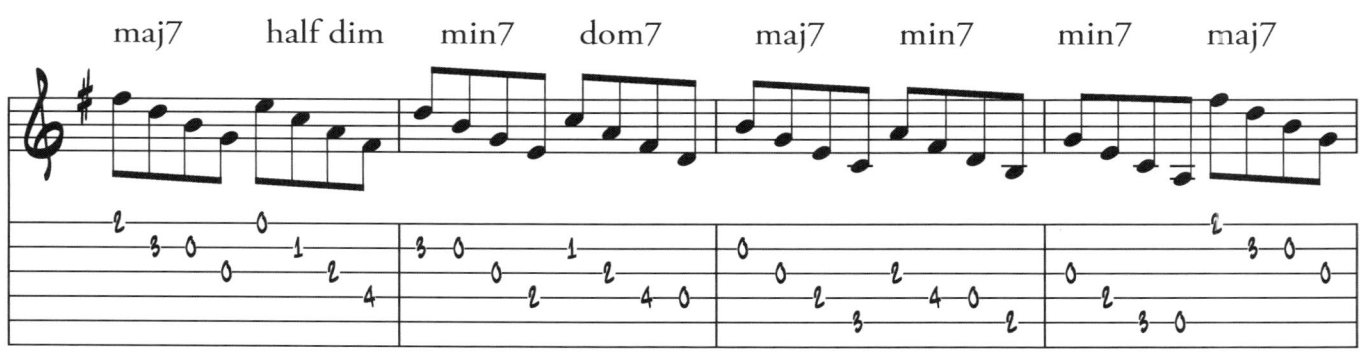

Descending

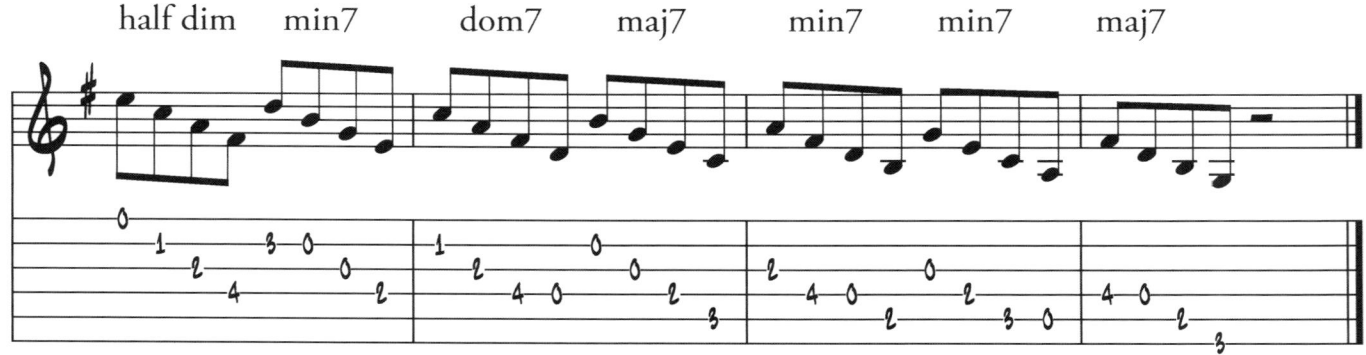

Permutation 2
Ascending & descending

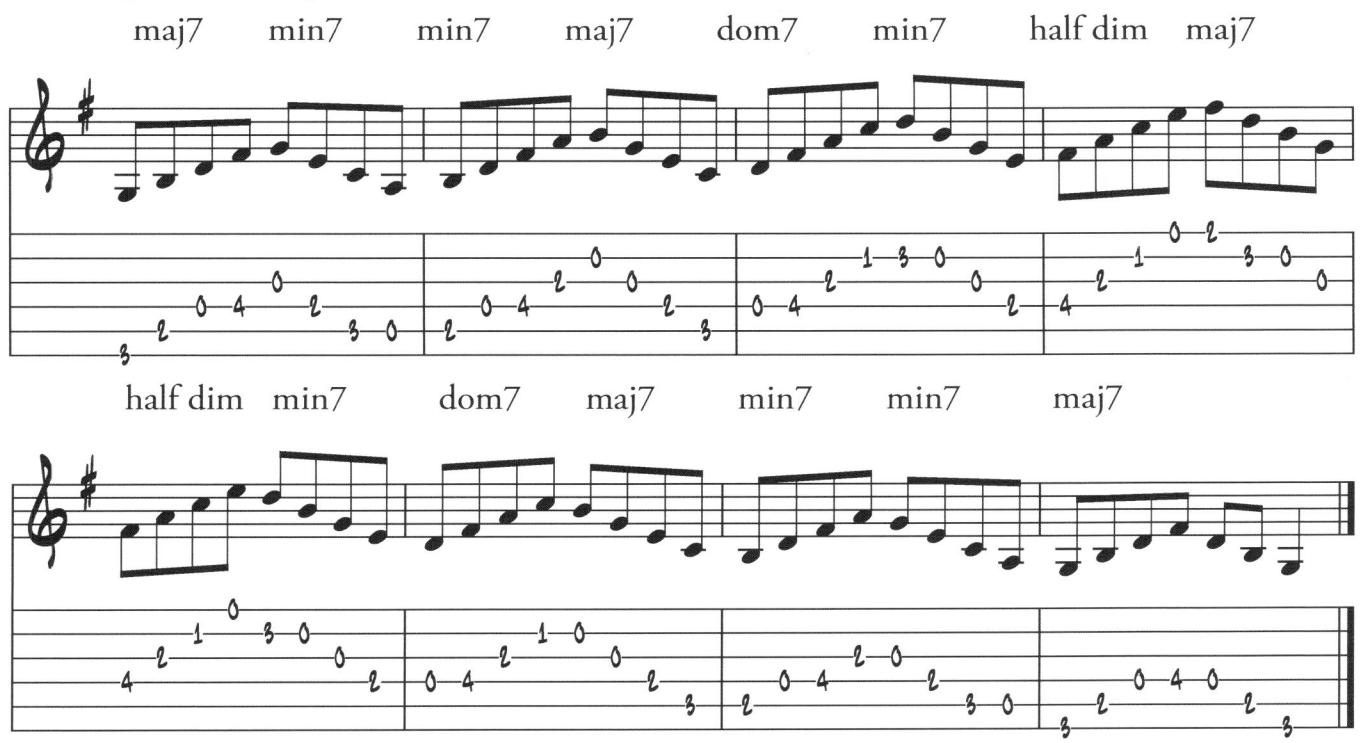

Permutation 3
Down the chord stepwise up the scale

3 Note Groupings

G major scale in triplet groupings
Ascending

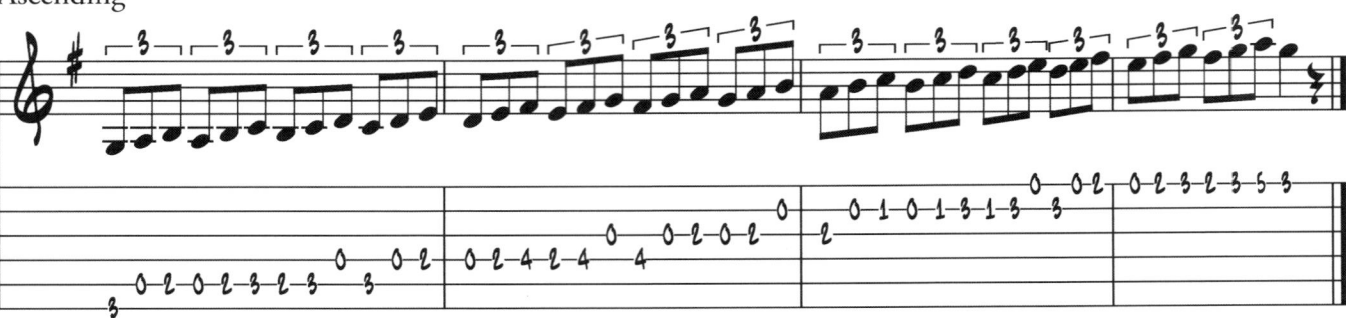

Descending

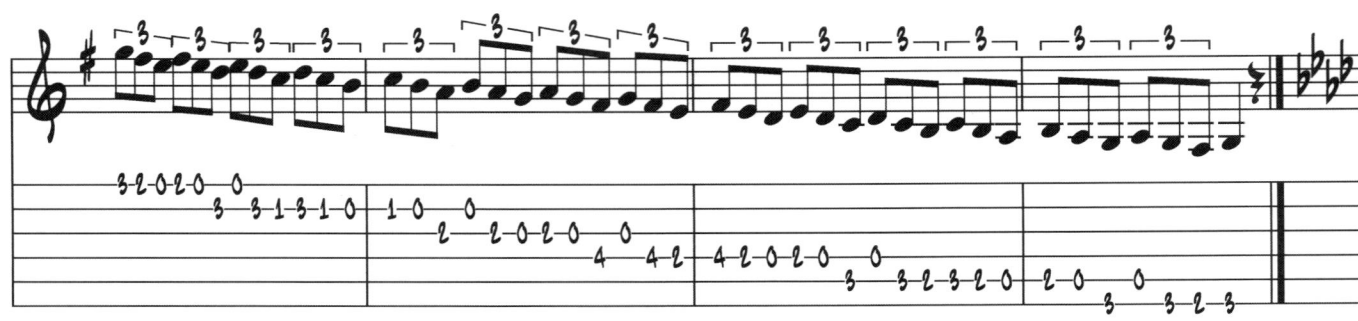

Scale studies in the key of Ab Major

Scales, Modes and Arpeggios over 2 octaves

Ab Major scale

Ab maj 7 arpeggio

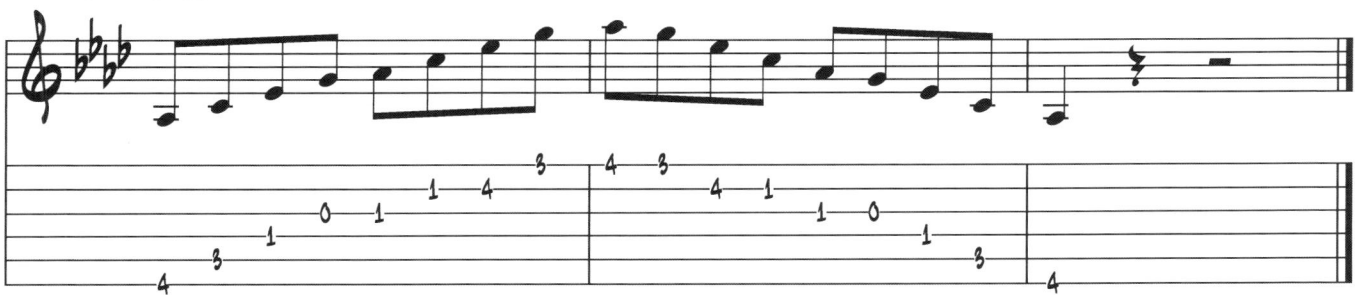

Bb Dorian scale

Bb min 7 arpeggio

C Phrygian scale

C min 7 arpeggio

Db Lydian scale

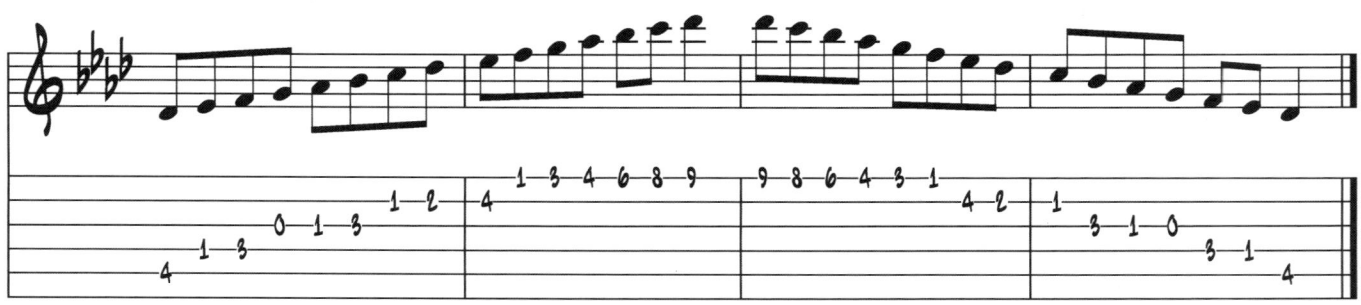

Db maj 7 arpeggio

Eb Mixolydian scale

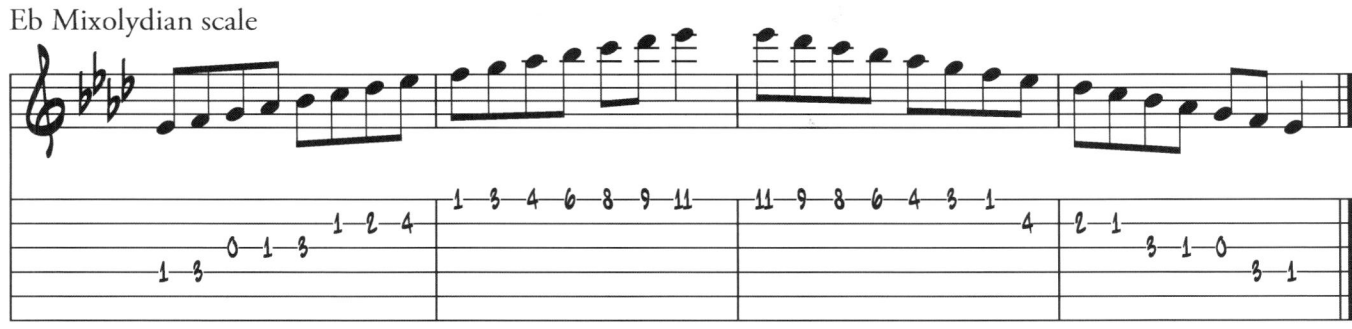

Eb 7 arpeggio

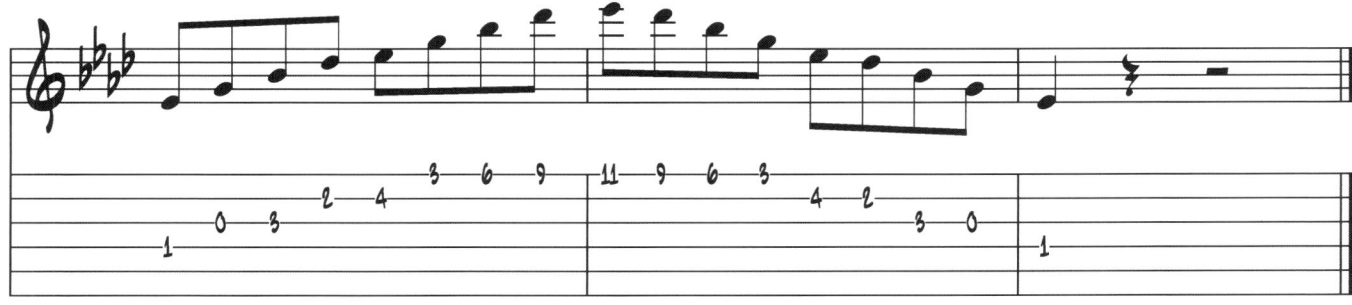

F Aeolian scale

F min7 arpeggio

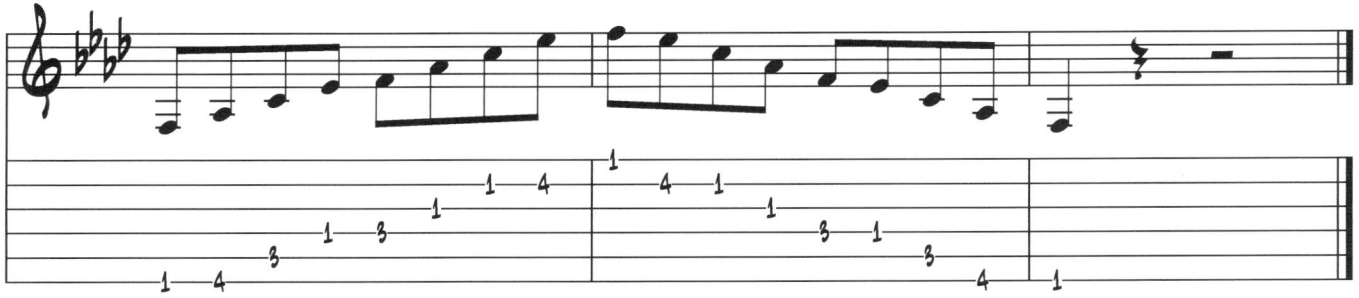

G Locrian scale

G min7 b5 arpeggio

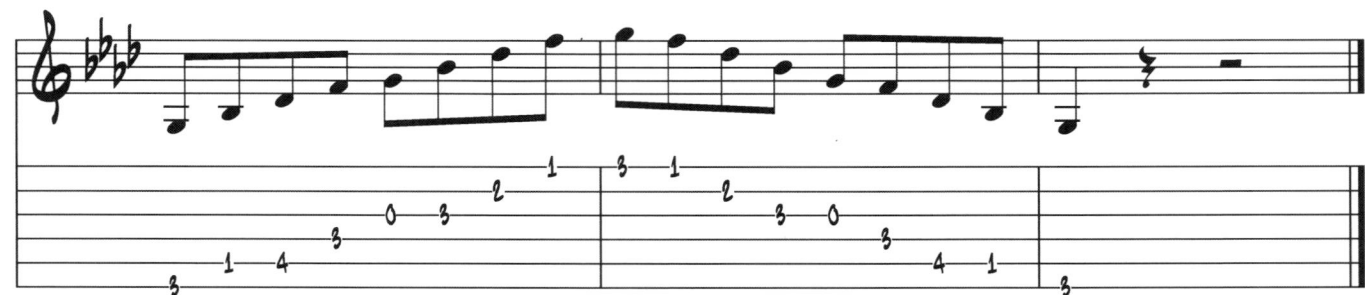

4 Note Scale Groupings

The following exercise outlines the use of 4 note groupings moving stepwise diatonically through the scale of Ab major.

For example, the 4 note grouping starts on the root note or 1st degree of the scale and progresses stepwise. The exercise then descends from the 2nd octave Ab back to the root.

Ascending

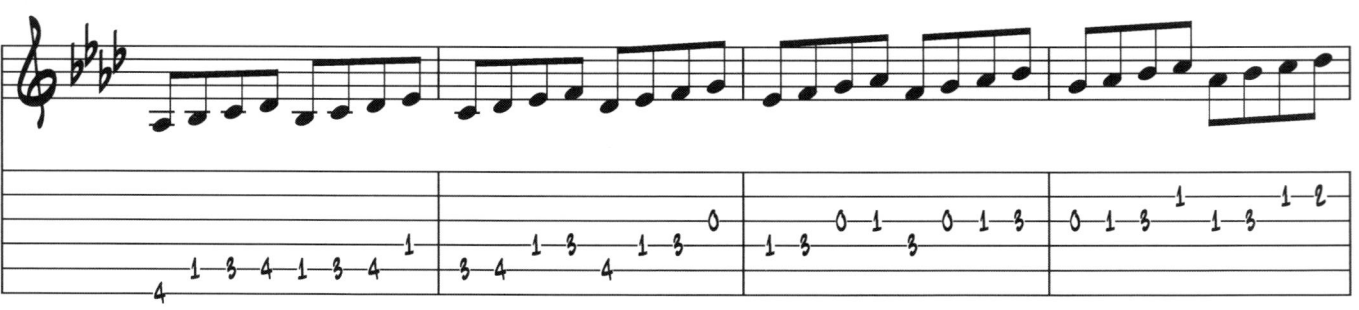

Descending

Permutation 2   Up & Down

As in the previous exercise the following exercise outlines the use of 4 note groupings moving stepwise diatonically through the scale of Ab major.

Notice in exercise #2 the 4 note grouping starts on the root note or 1st degree of the scale and progresses stepwise. In this example we descend when we hit the 5th note in the sequence eg. descending from the 2nd 4 note grouping.

Ascending

Descending

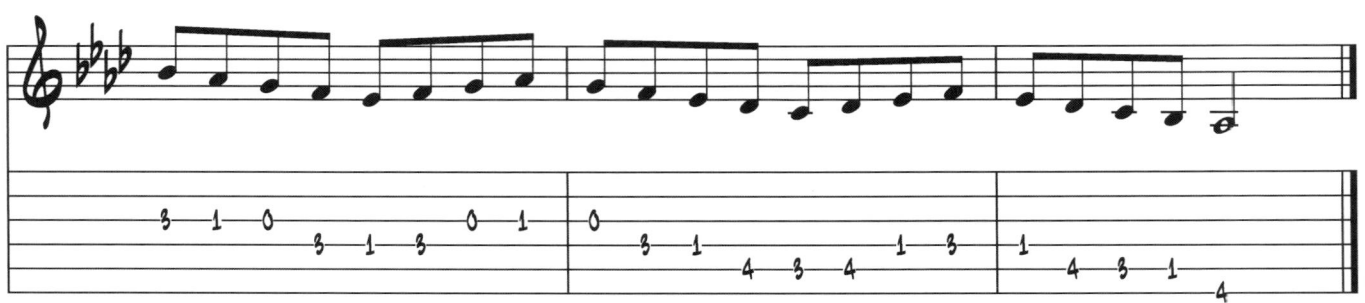

Broken Thirds

Ascending

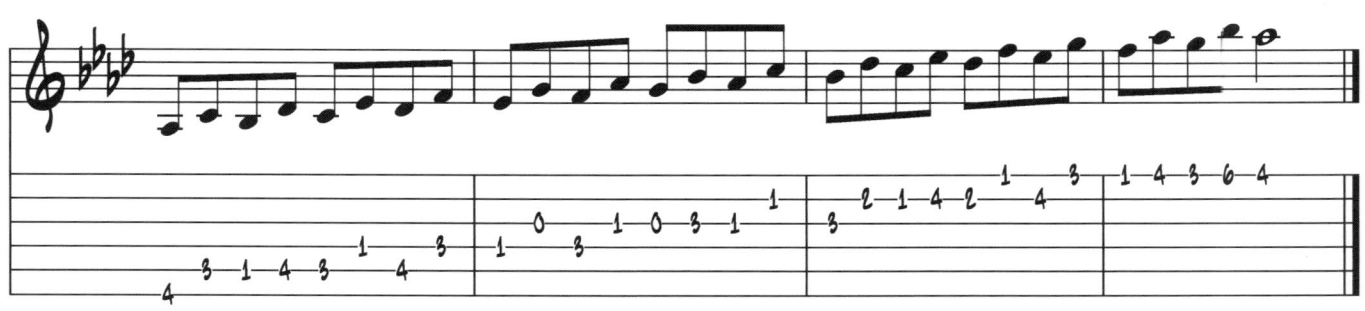

Descending

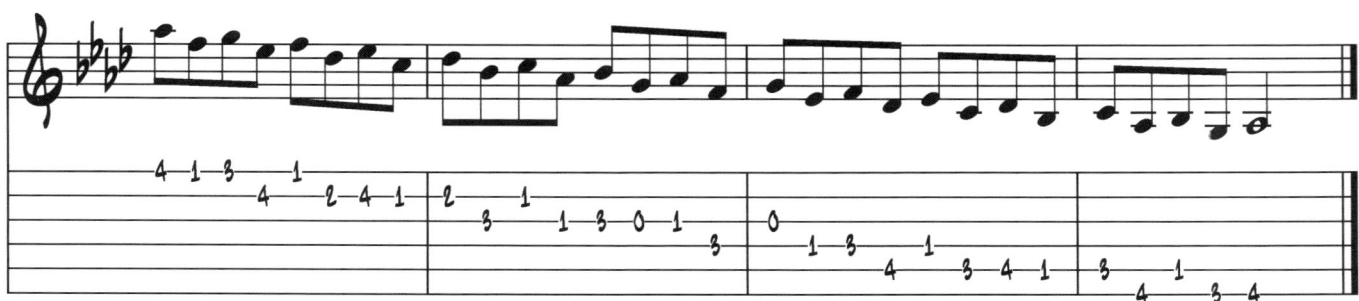

4 Note Groupings Diatonic Triads

4 Note Groupings Diatonic 7th Chords

Permutation 2
Ascending & descending

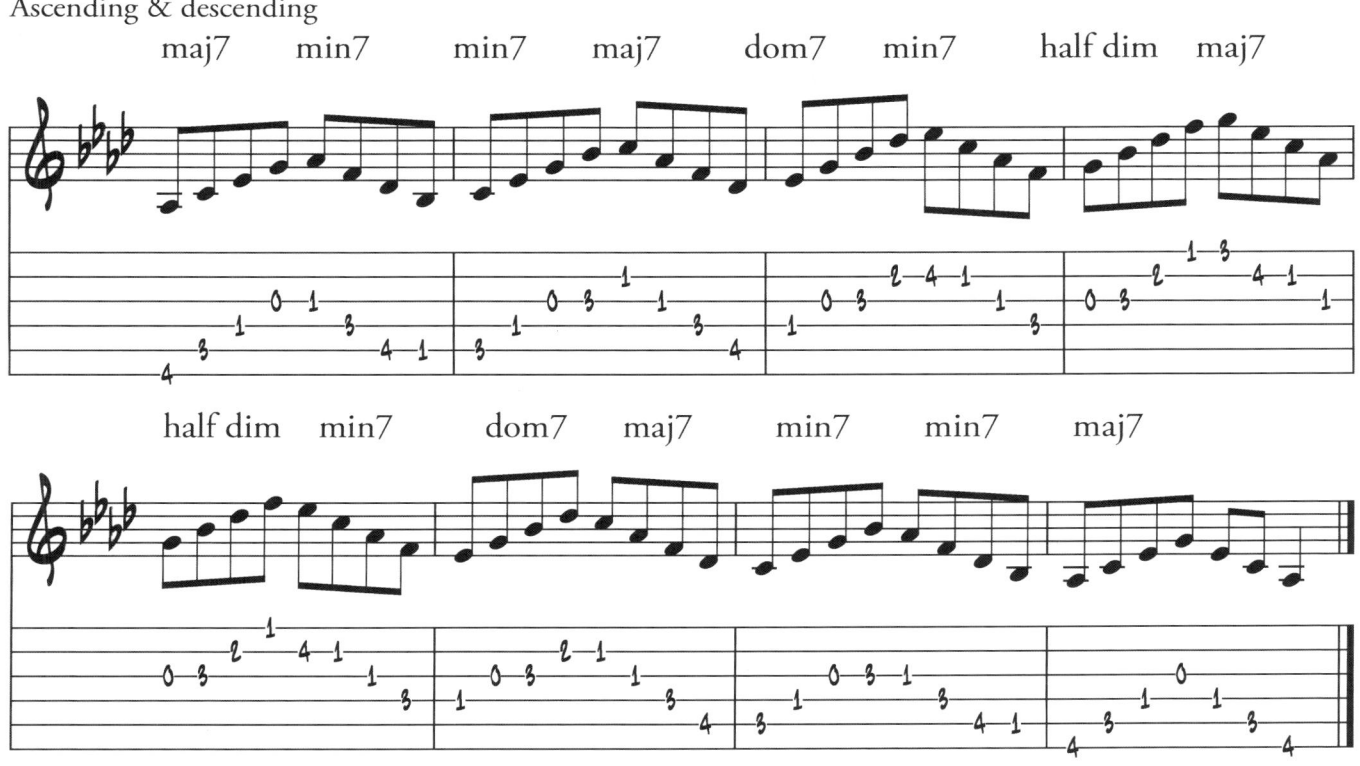

Permutation 3
Down the chord stepwise up the scale

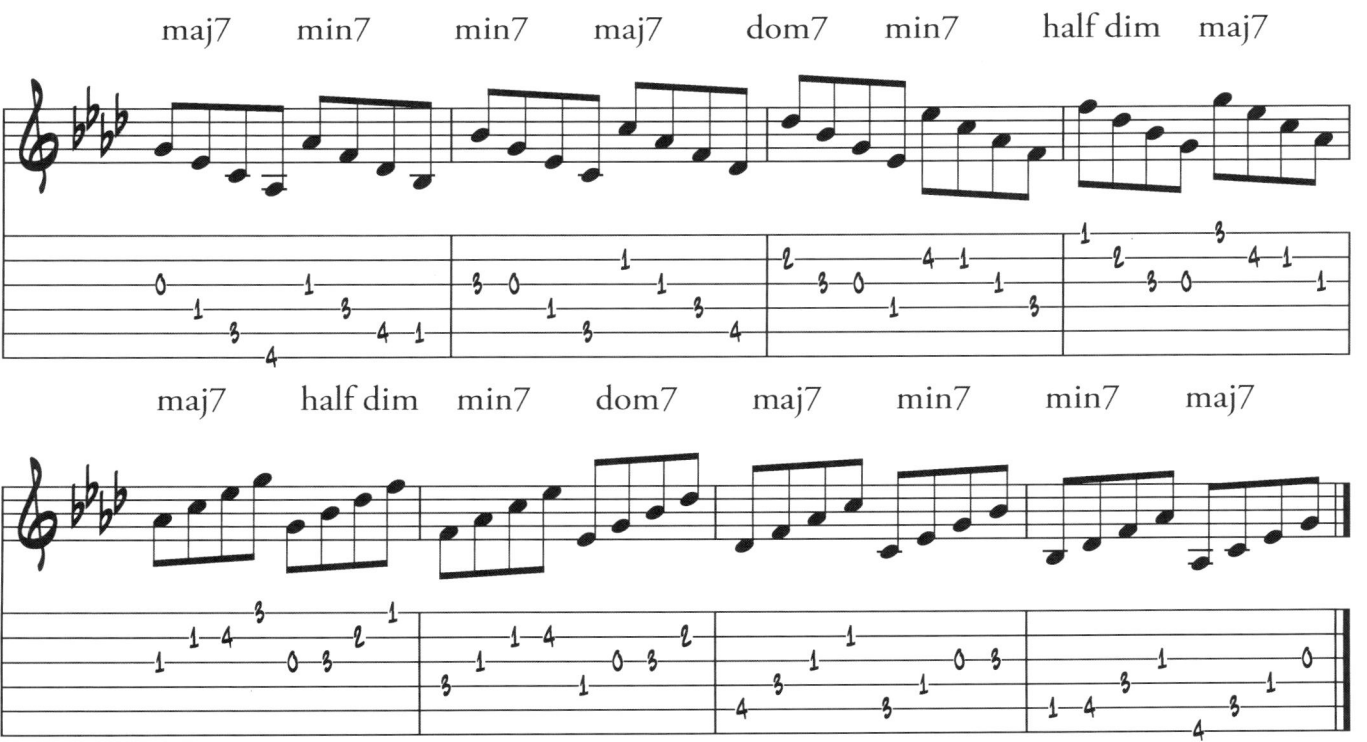

3 Note Groupings

Ab major scale in triplet groupings
Ascending

Descending

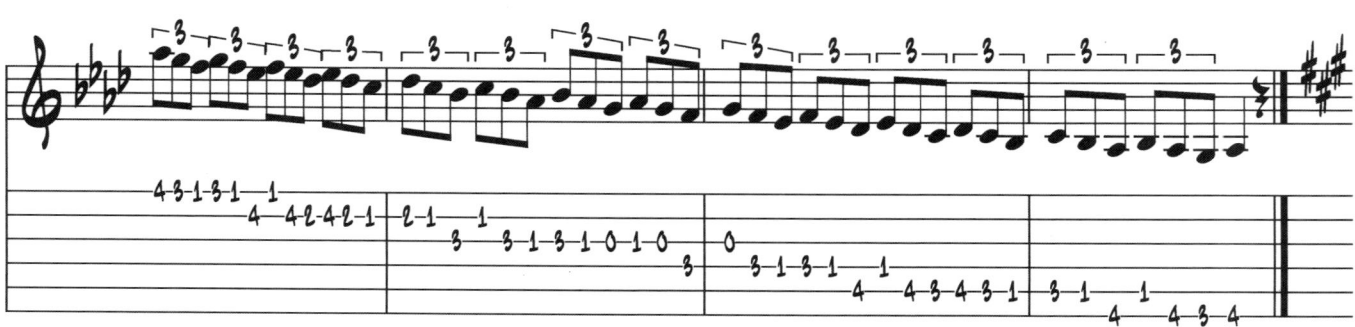

Scale studies in the key of A Major

Scales, Modes and Arpeggios over 2 octaves

A Major scale

A maj 7 arpeggio

B Dorian scale

B min 7 arpeggio

C# Phrygian scale

C# min 7 arpeggio

D Lydian scale

D maj 7 arpeggio

E Mixolydian scale

E 7 arpeggio

F# Aeolian scale

F# min7 arpeggio

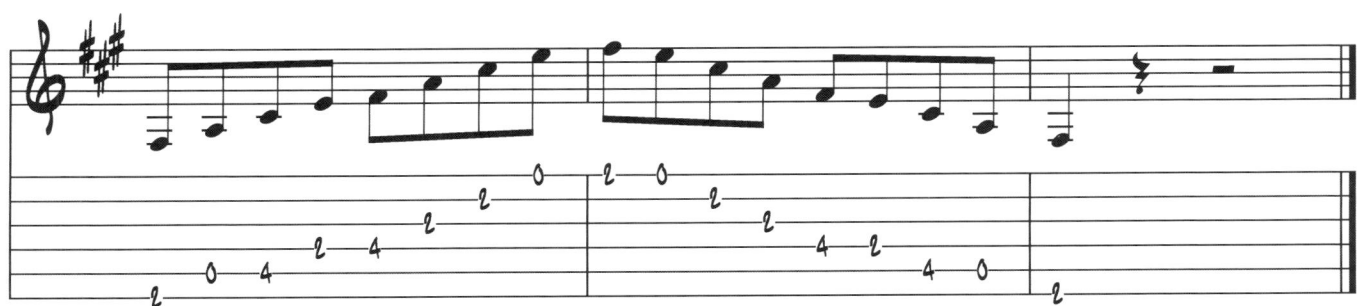

G# Locrian scale

G# min7 b5 arpeggio

4 Note Scale Groupings

The following exercise outlines the use of 4 note groupings moving stepwise diatonically through the scale of A major.

For example, the 4 note grouping starts on the root note or 1st degree of the scale and progresses stepwise. The exercise then descends from the 2nd octave A back to the root.

Ascending

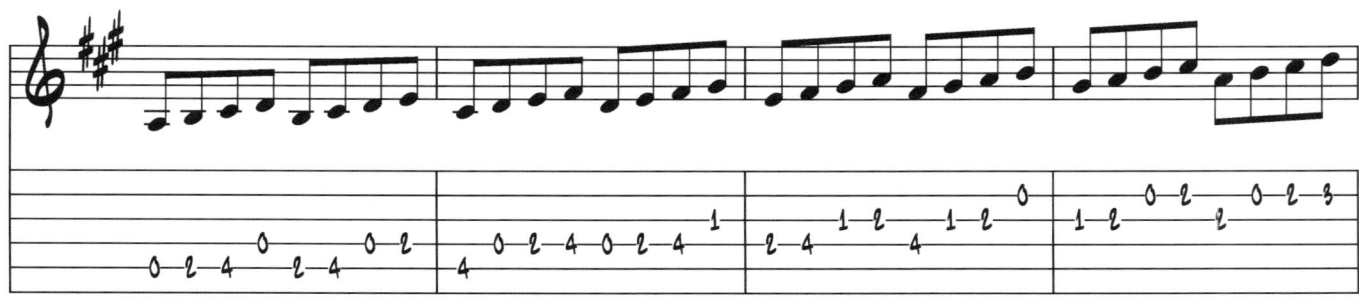

Descending

Permutation 2   Up & Down

As in the previous exercise the following exercise outlines the use of 4 note groupings moving stepwise diatonically through the scale of A major.

Notice in exercise #2 the 4 note grouping starts on the root note or 1st degree of the scale and progresses stepwise. In this example we descend when we hit the 5th note in the sequence eg. descending from the 2nd 4 note grouping.

Ascending

Descending

Broken Thirds

Ascending

Descending

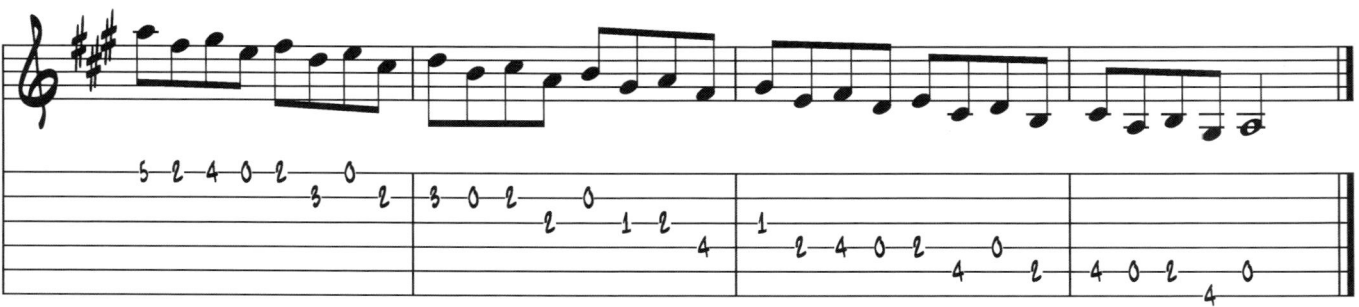

4 Note Groupings Diatonic Triads

Ascending 1351

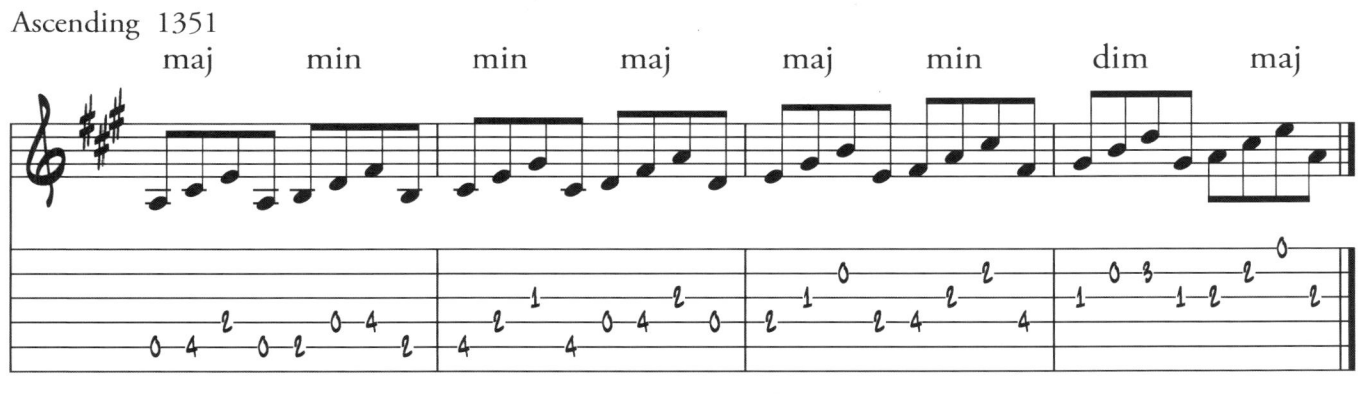

Descending 1351

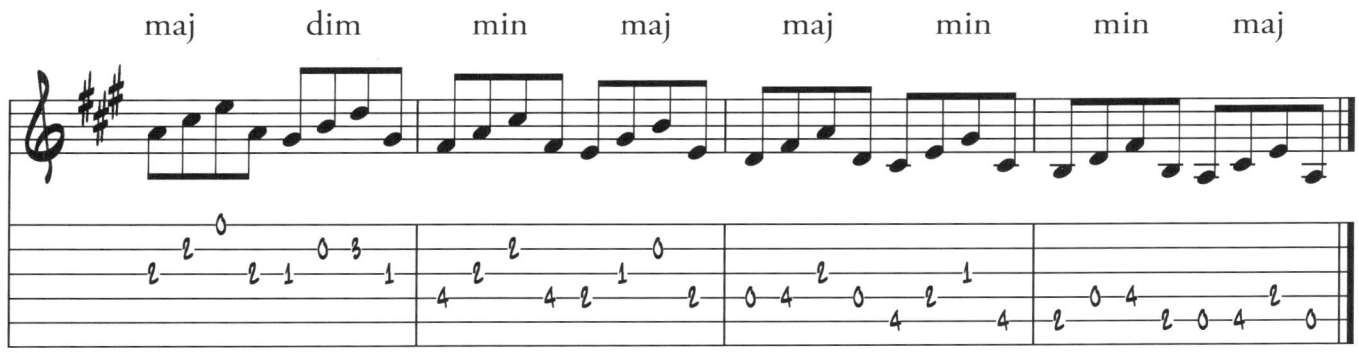

Ascending 1531

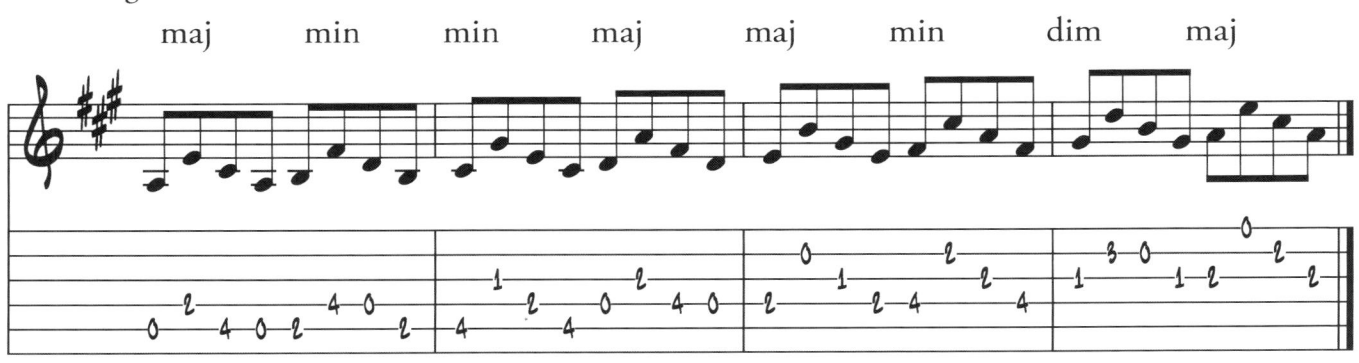

Descending 1531

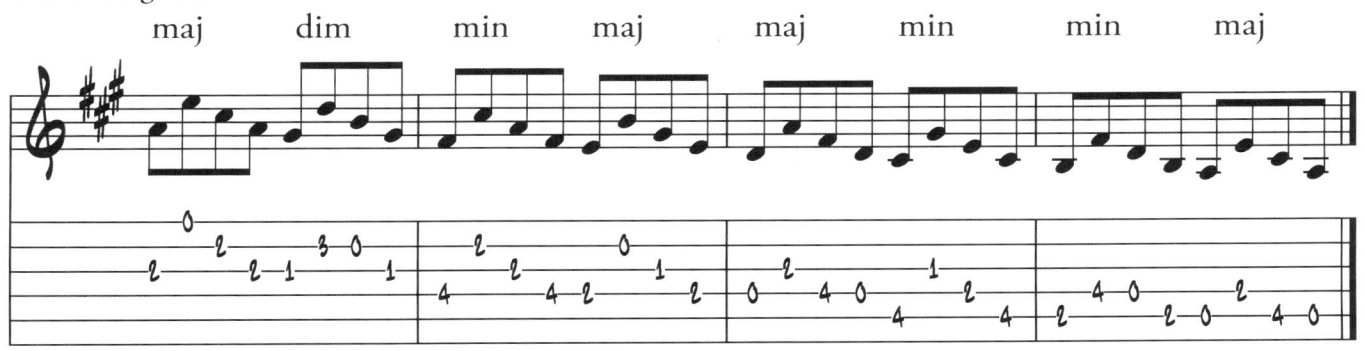

4 Note Groupings Diatonic 7th Chords

Ascending

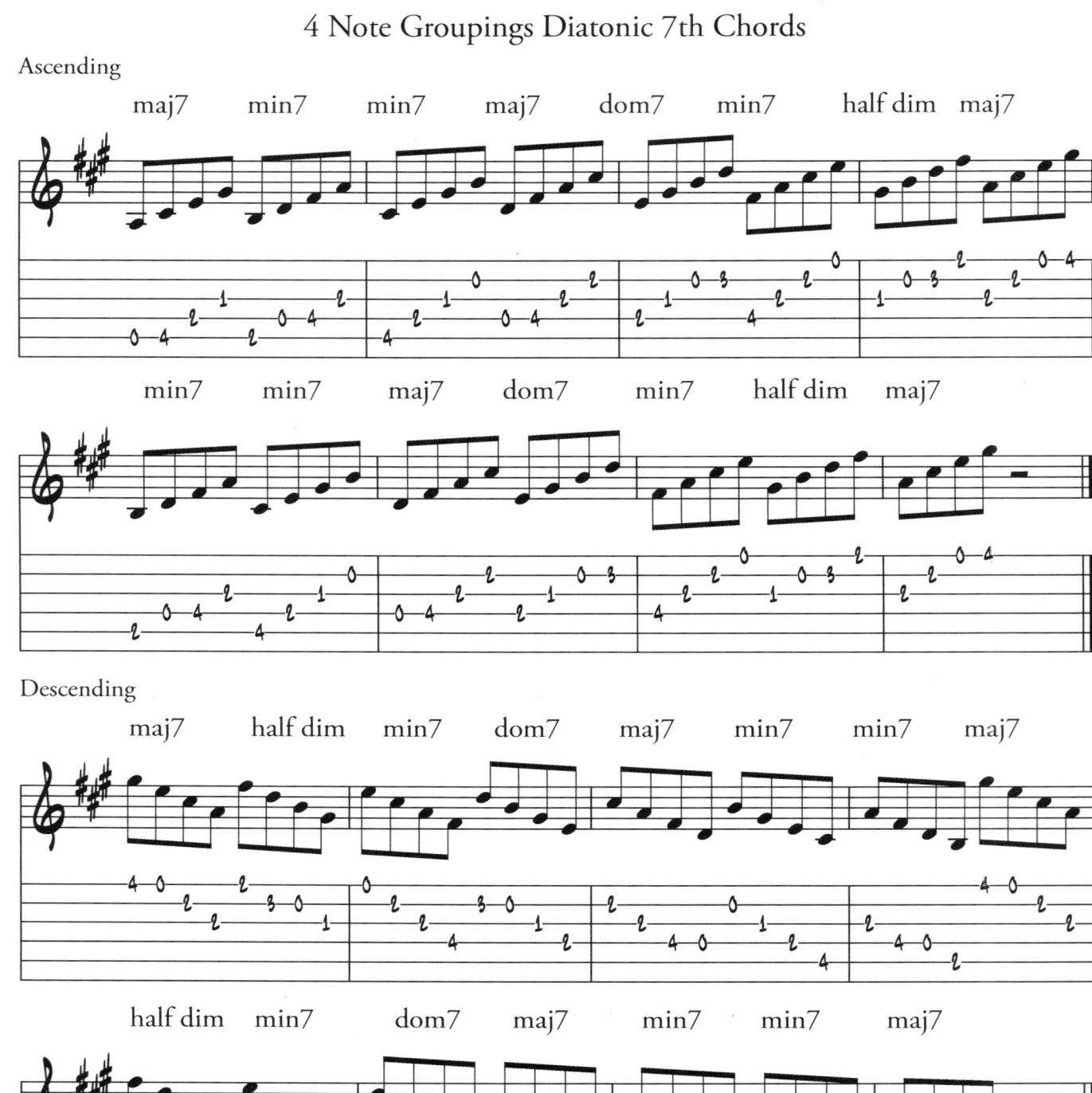

Descending

Permutation 2
Ascending & descending

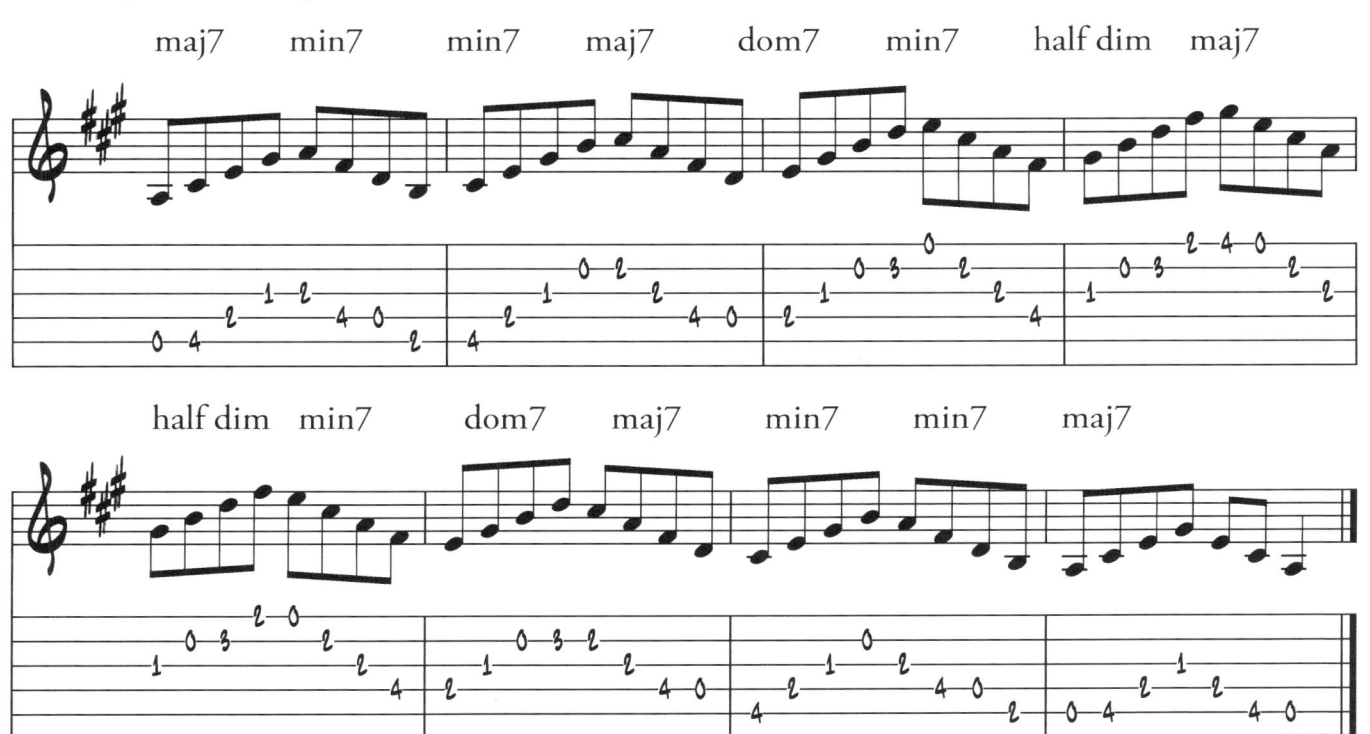

Permutation 3
Down the chord stepwise up the scale

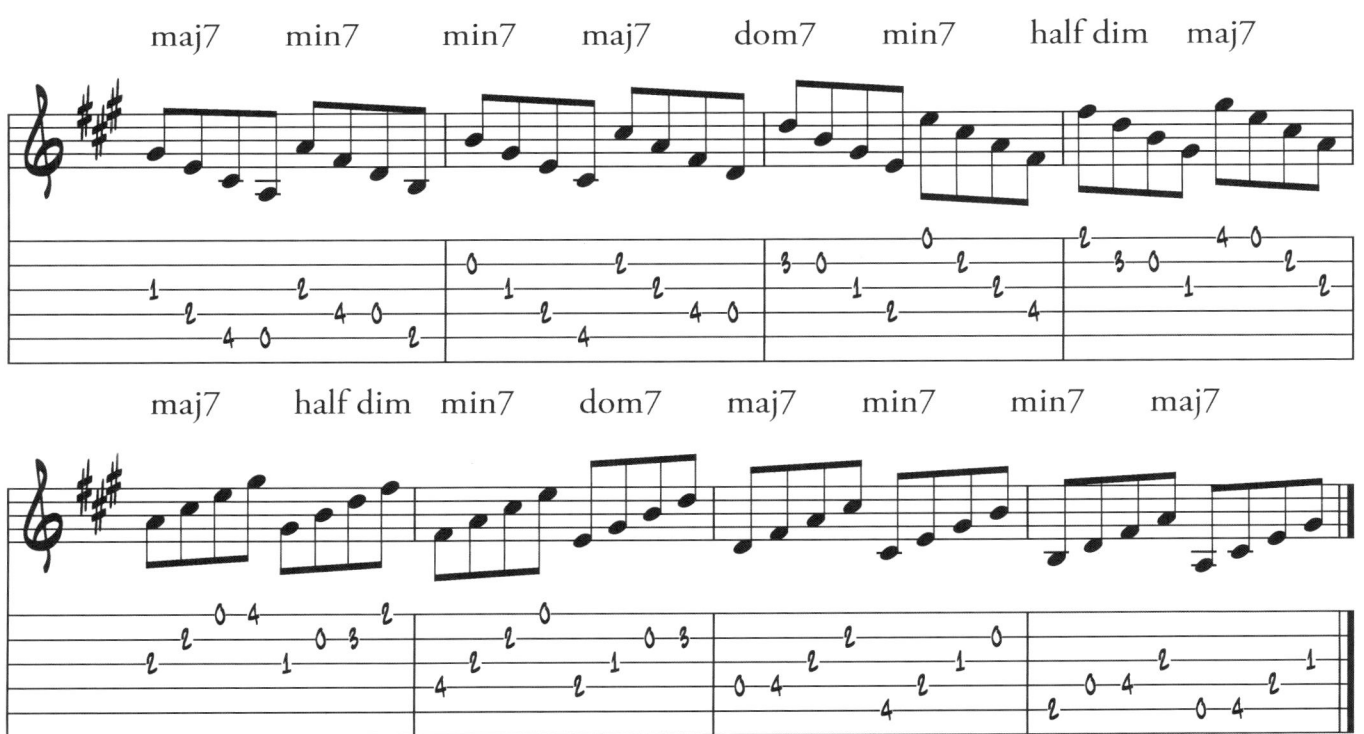

3 Note Groupings

A major scale in triplet groupings

Ascending

Descending

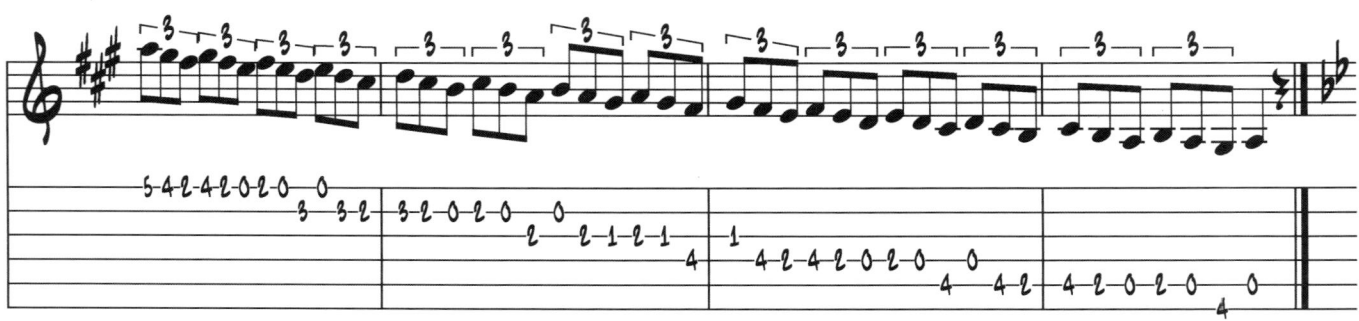

Scale studies in the key of Bb Major

Scales, Modes and Arpeggios over 2 octaves

Bb Major scale

Bb maj 7 arpeggio

C Dorian scale

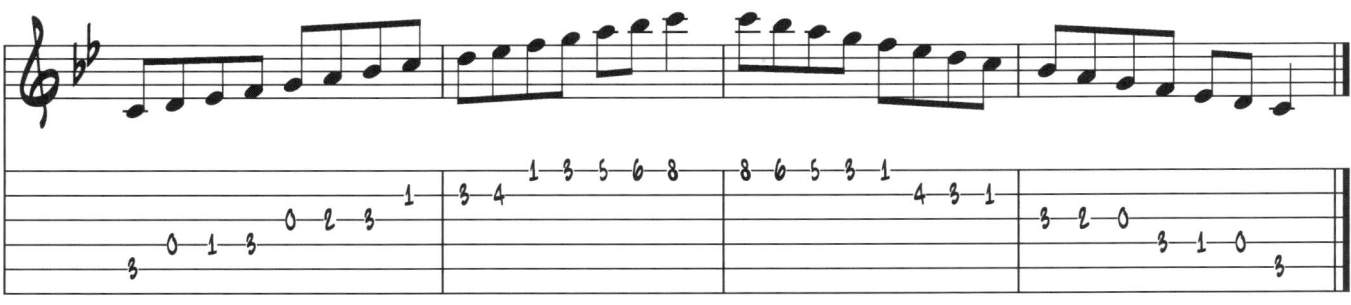

C min 7 arpeggio

D Phrygian scale

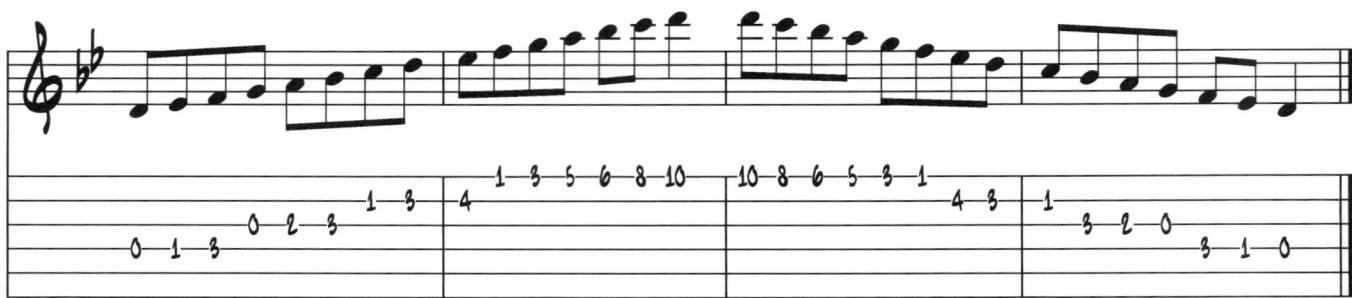

D min 7 arpeggio

Eb Lydian scale

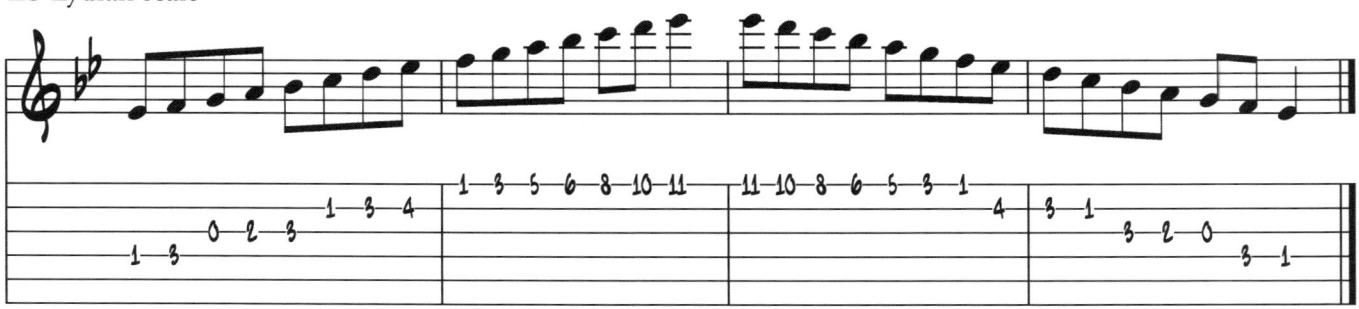

Eb maj 7 arpeggio

F Mixolydian scale

F 7 arpeggio

G Aeolian scale

G min7 arpeggio

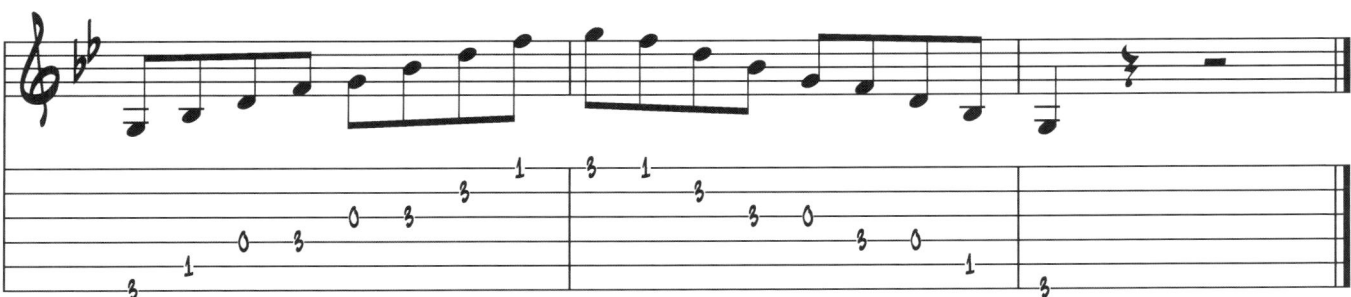

A Locrian scale

A min7 b5 arpeggio

4 Note Scale Groupings

The following exercise outlines the use of 4 note groupings moving stepwise diatonically through the scale of Bb major.

For example, the 4 note grouping starts on the root note or 1st degree of the scale and progresses stepwise. The exercise then descends from the 2nd octave Bb back to the root.

Ascending

Descending

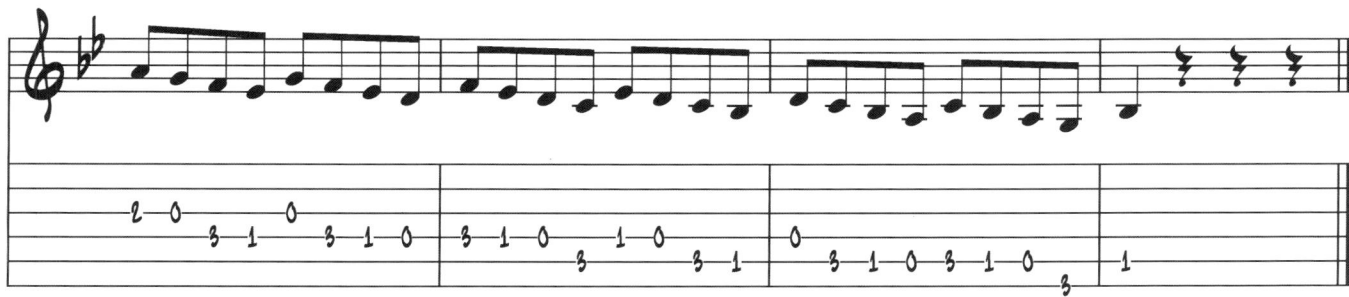

Permutation 2   Up & Down

As in the previous exercise the following exercise outlines the use of 4 note groupings moving stepwise diatonically through the scale of Bb major.

Notice in exercise #2 the 4 note grouping starts on the root note or 1st degree of the scale and progresses stepwise. In this example we descend when we hit the 5th note in the sequence eg. descending from the 2nd 4 note grouping.

Ascending

Descending

Broken Thirds

Ascending

Descending

4 Note Groupings Diatonic Triads

Ascending 1351

Descending 1351

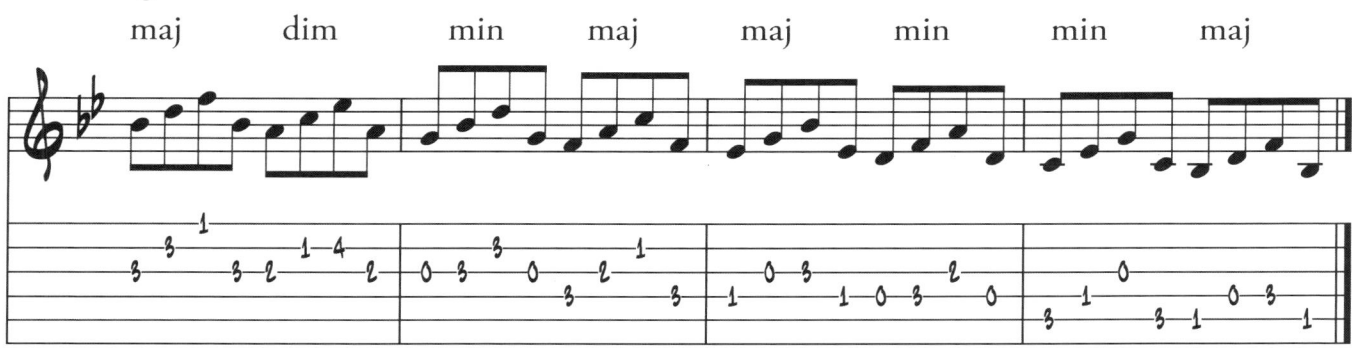

Ascending 1531

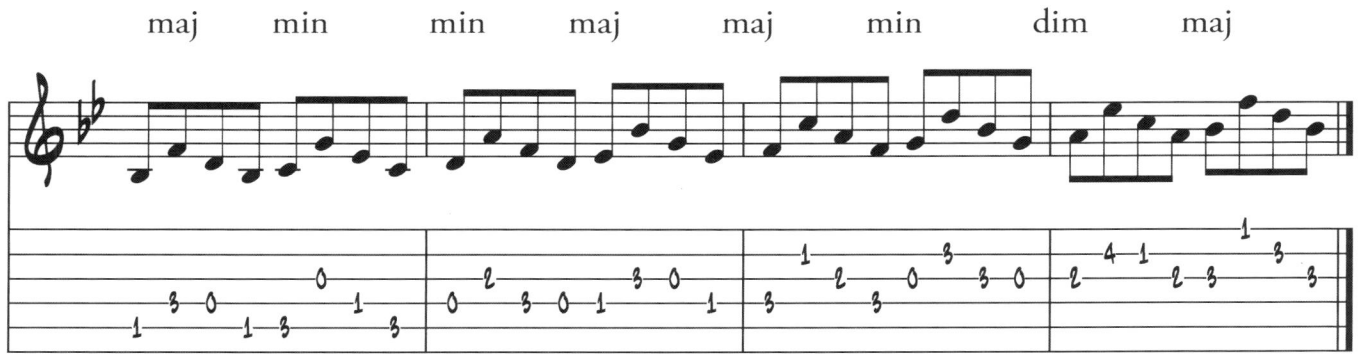

Descending 1531

4 Note Groupings Diatonic 7th Chords

Ascending

Descending

Permutation 2
Ascending & descending

maj7   min7   min7   maj7   dom7   min7   half dim   maj7

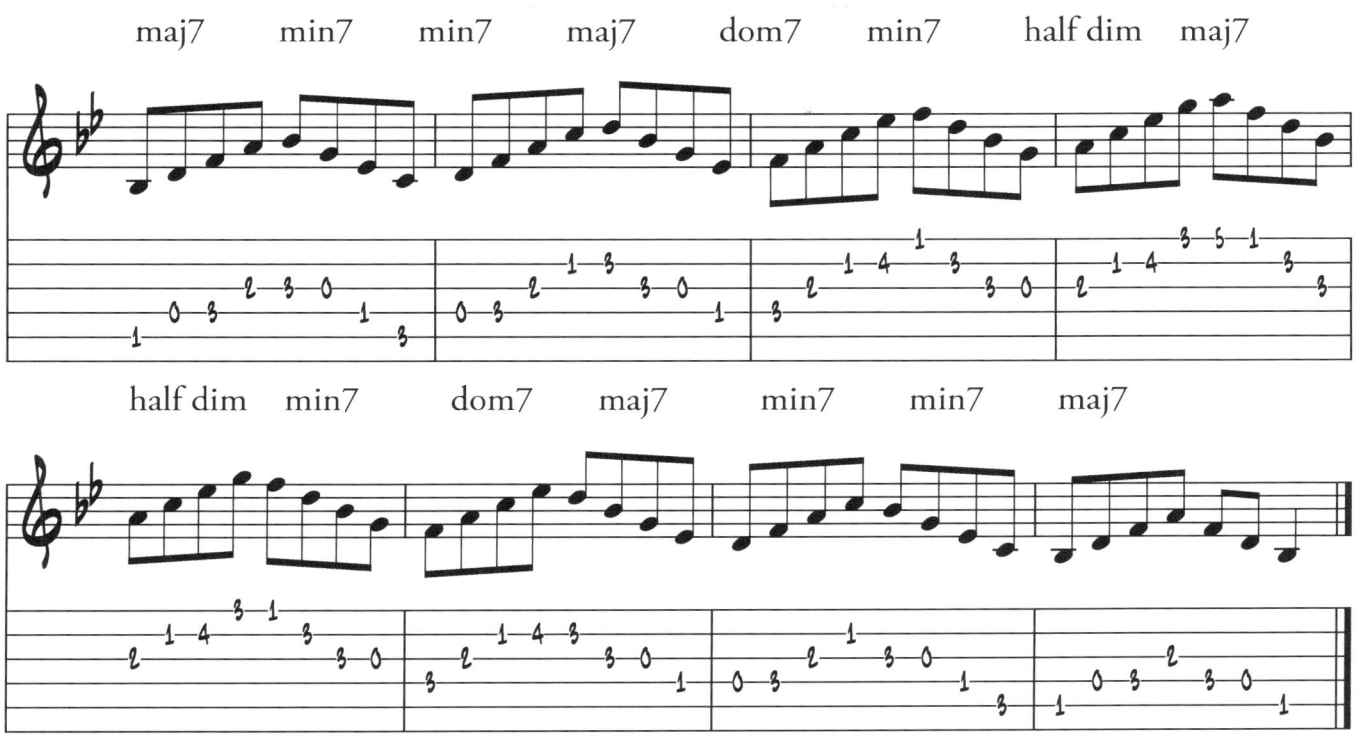

half dim   min7   dom7   maj7   min7   min7   maj7

Permutation 3
Down the chord stepwise up the scale

maj7   min7   min7   maj7   dom7   min7   half dim   maj7

maj7   half dim   min7   dom7   maj7   min7   min7   maj7

3 Note Groupings

Bb major scale in triplet groupings
Ascending

Descending

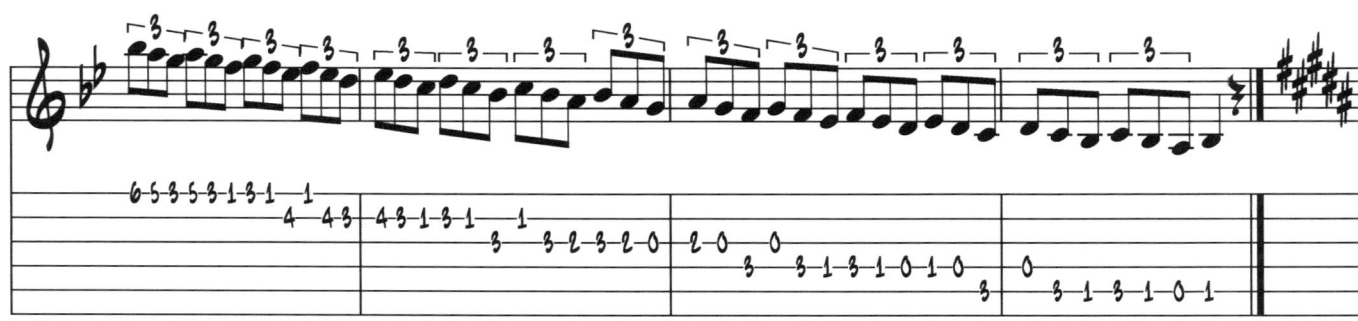

Scale studies in the key of B Major

Scales, Modes and Arpeggios over 2 octaves

B Major scale

B maj 7 arpeggio

C# Dorian scale

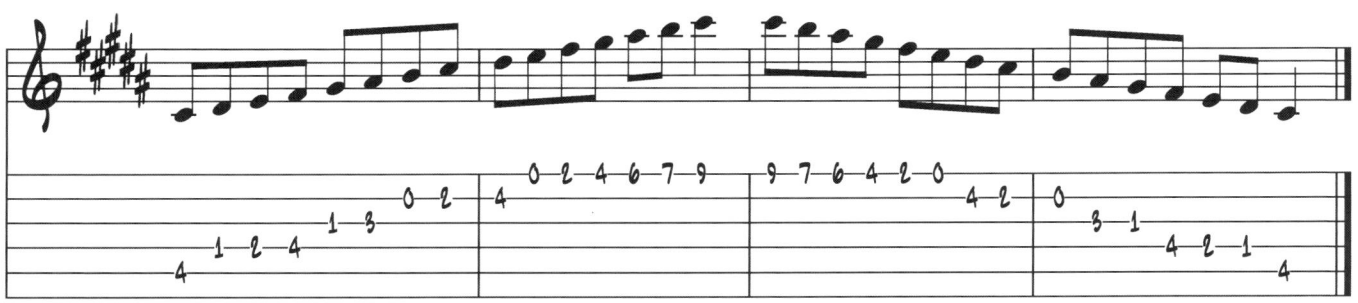

C# min 7 arpeggio

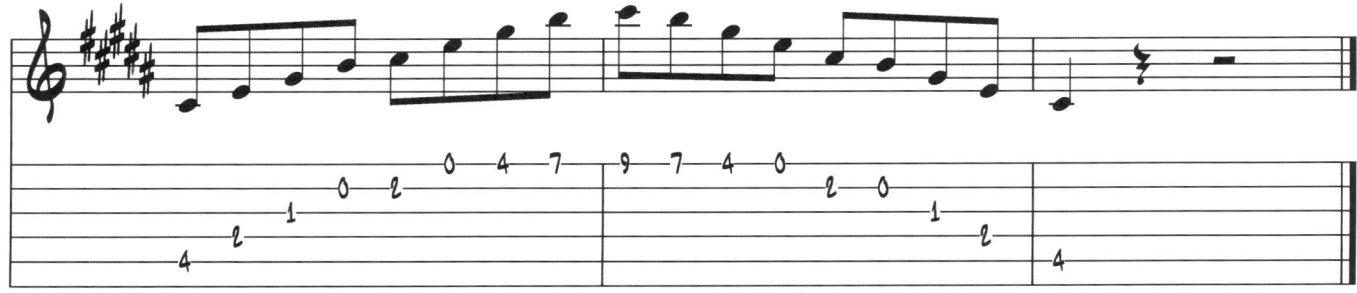

D# Phrygian scale

D# min 7 arpeggio

E Lydian scale

E maj 7 arpeggio

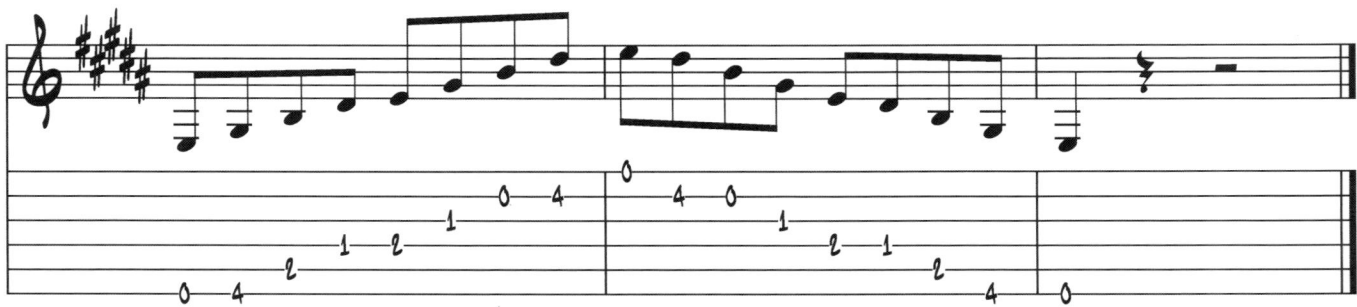

F# Mixolydian scale

F# 7 arpeggio

G# Aeolian scale

G# min7 arpeggio

A# Locrian scale

A# min7 b5 arpeggio

4 Note Scale Groupings

The following exercise outlines the use of 4 note groupings moving stepwise diatonically through the scale of B major.

For example, the 4 note grouping starts on the root note or 1st degree of the scale and progresses stepwise. The exercise then descends from the 2nd octave B back to the root.

Ascending

Descending

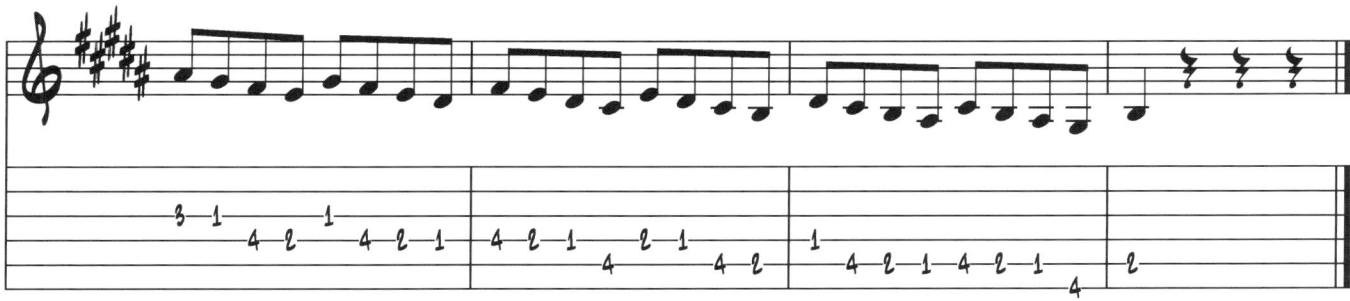

Permutation 2   Up & Down

As in the previous exercise the following exercise outlines the use of 4 note groupings moving stepwise diatonically through the scale of B major.

Notice in exercise #2 the 4 note grouping starts on the root note or 1st degree of the scale and progresses stepwise. In this example we descend when we hit the 5th note in the sequence eg. descending from the 2nd 4 note grouping.

Ascending

Descending

Broken Thirds

Ascending

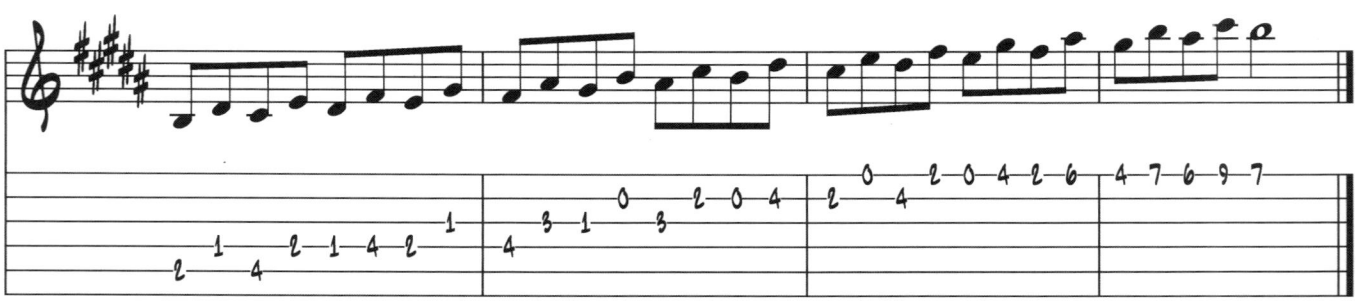

Descending

4 Note Groupings Diatonic Triads

4 Note Groupings Diatonic 7th Chords

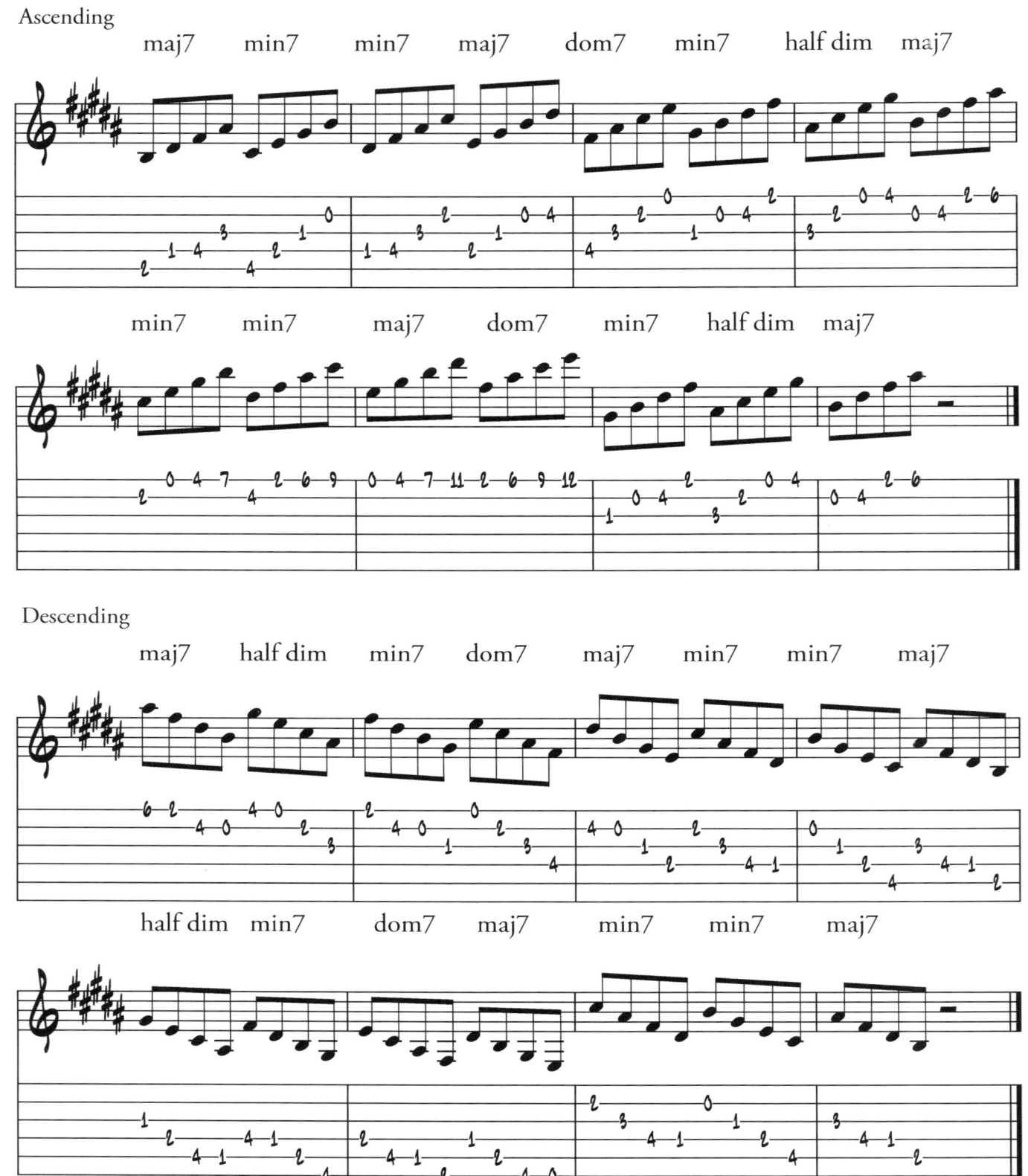

Permutation 2
Ascending & descending

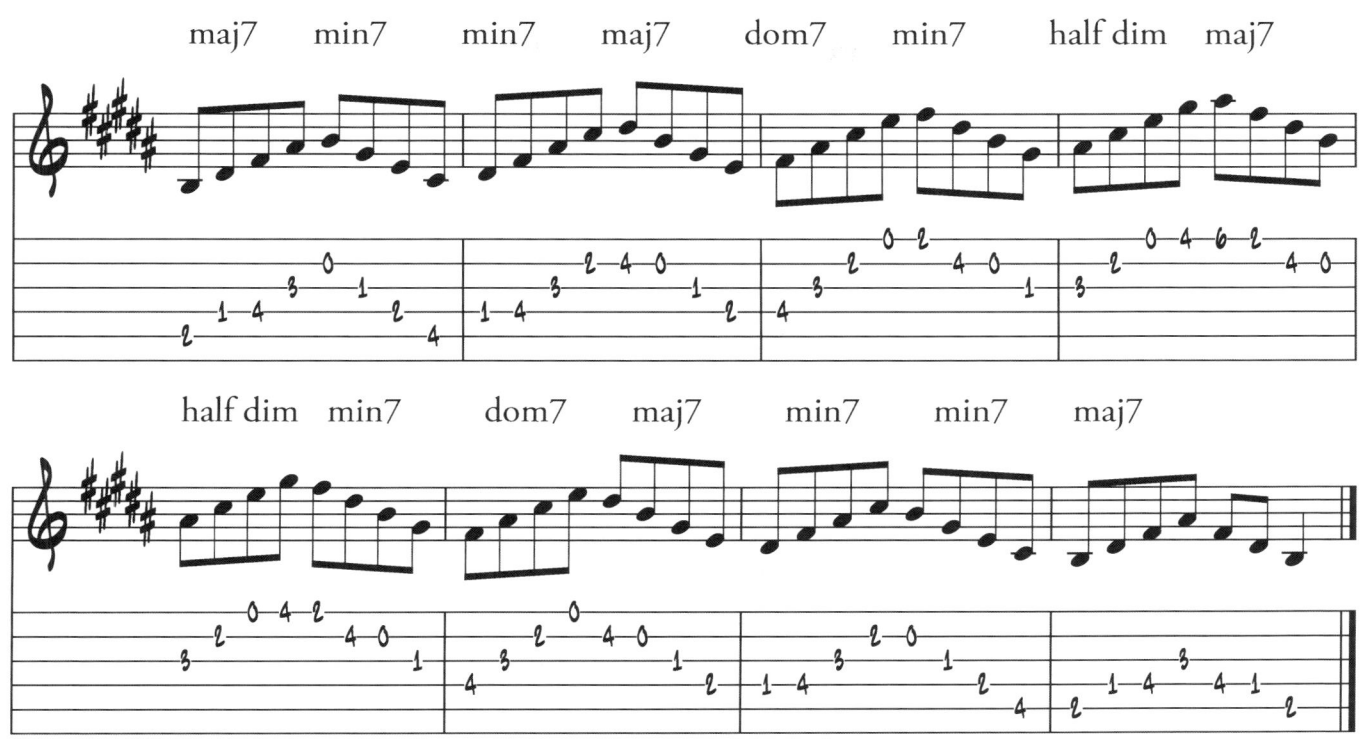

Permutation 3
Down the chord stepwise up the scale

3 Note Groupings

B major scale in triplet groupings
Ascending

Descending

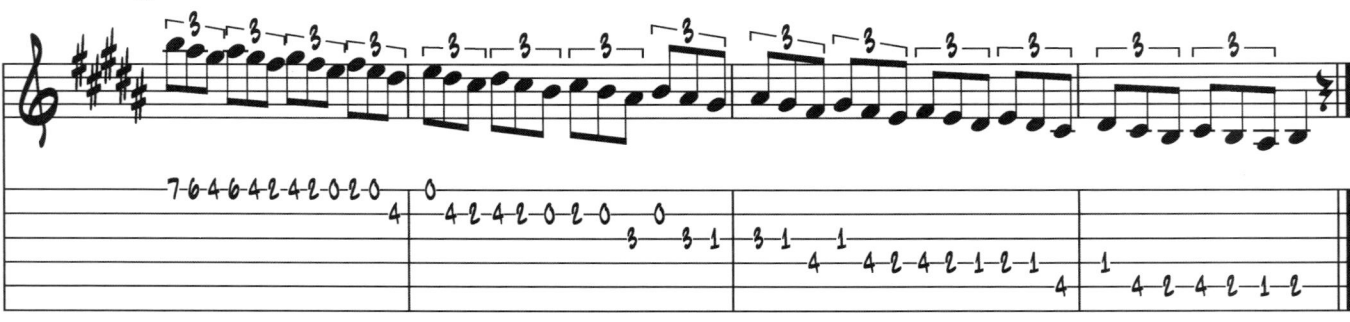

IN CONCLUSION ......

It has been a vast amount of work and dedicated practice that brings the guitarist to the last page of this book having covered all the examples within.

It has been the aim of the " Jazz Guitar Workshop " guitar tab book series to give the aspiring jazz guitarist a solid grounding in how to develop a dedicated daily practice routine.

Having covered the material in this book you are now well on your way to finding your own voice as a guitarist and as a musician.

For those of you reading the book that are not familiar with reading treble clef, all examples inside the book have been supplied with guitar tab and treble clef, use this as a tool to learn to read the treble clef.

There are many opportunities for the reading musician.

Practice the exercises until they become familiar striving for good tone, time and articulation but most importantly - Listen to as much music as you can, Listen to the masters.

The objective has been to make the material for the student as easy to absorb as possible,

as a confidance building mechanism.

Your thoughts and comments are important to us and assist us in providing future generations of musicians with quality educational material.

Please send youre thoughts or comments to info@jazzguitarworks.com

Other books by Robert Green

Jazz Guitar Workshop - 12 key Jazz Guitar Workout.

Coming Soon.
Jazz Guitar Workshop Book II

Follow us on the web at

Waterfallpublishinghouse.com

Jazzguitarworks.com

Printed in Great Britain
by Amazon

16327017R00075